Investment Portfolio Selection Using Goal Programming

Investment Portfolio Selection Using Goal Programming: An Approach to Making Investment Decisions

By

Dr. Rania Ahmed Azmi

CAMBRIDGE SCHOLARS

PUBLISHING

Investment Portfolio Selection Using Goal Programming:
An Approach to Making Investment Decisions,
by Dr. Rania Ahmed Azmi

This book first published 2013

Cambridge Scholars Publishing

12 Back Chapman Street, Newcastle upon Tyne, NE6 2XX, UK

British Library Cataloguing in Publication Data
A catalogue record for this book is available from the British Library

ISBN (10): 1-4438-4653-8, ISBN (13): 978-1-4438-4653-0

This book is dedicated to my mom and dad:
Mrs. Fadia Abdel Salam
Eng. Ahmed Azmi

Their unconditional love, understanding and support in all that I have done are the keys of all my achievements and they are responsible for every good thing I have ever done.

"He that wants money, means, and content, is without three good friends."
—William Shakespeare (1564-1616)

CONTENTS

LIST OF ILLUSTRATIONS

LIST OF TABLES

PREFACE

This book suggests new scientific frameworks for investment decision making and portfolio selection and analysis that can be utilised equally by practitioners and academics. The main contributions here proposed are the application of Goal Programming to portfolio selection, the development and testing of new weighting schemes and a novel approach in extending Goal Programming models to incorporate several factors for global portfolio selection and analysis.

This book is thus intended to contribute to the theory of portfolio selection by using Goal Programming and its variants. In particular, it aims at providing the decision maker (whether an individual or institutional investor, policy maker, etc.), who is usually burdened with achieving multiple (often conflicting) objectives under complex environmental constraints, with a new scientific framework to accomplish goals and satisfy preferences.

Accordingly, this book is structured as follows:

Following the first chapter, which introduces Goal Programming for real-world decision making, chapter two presents a thorough literature review of Goal Programming for Portfolio Selection. The chapter starts with overviews of the use of multi-criteria decision analysis in portfolio selection and the importance of Goal Programming. The chapter also discusses portfolio selection using Goal Programming in the light of various theoretical and practical developments.

With these themes as a background, chapter three provides a general overview of the main methodologies used in this book; namely, Goal Programming, Markowitz, Konno's model, Sharpe and Treynor methodologies. Illustrations are provided throughout this chapter for convenience and ease of use regarding the mathematical models.

This leads on to chapter four, where the first experiments are framed in order to select a portfolio of mutual funds from two different markets—developed and emerging—with two different time periods, using Goal Programming, Sharpe and Treynor methods. The chapter's results have certain implications for the Goal Programming methodology as it is utilised in crisis time (the experiment in the UK market) and in regular time (the experiment in Egypt's market).

Chapter five builds on chapter four in terms of applying the same methodologies, but in selecting a portfolio of stocks. Some interesting results are reported.

The portfolio selection experiments with applications to mutual funds (chapter four) and stocks (chapter five) show that Goal Programming could be used effectively for selecting a portfolio's constituents. Deciding on the constituents' proportions is a subsequent important task. Accordingly, chapter six provides many choices for weighting schemes in order to obtain portfolio constituent proportions. The chapter explores these weighting schemes via experiments on mutual funds and stocks.

Building on the results reported for the experiments in chapters four through six, chapter seven goes beyond return-risk-based portfolio selection and attempts to select portfolios based on extended factors that closely reflect the nature of the portfolio problem in today's world. It therefore considers several factors—such as regional preferences and macroeconomic factors—for the international mutual fund portfolio selection problem. Interesting results are reported and thorough analysis is provided.

The book concludes in chapters eight and nine with a discussion of various further perspectives and thoughts regarding the various topics that have been covered.

I hope the reader will enjoy exploring the suggested investment decision-making framework and will make use of the knowledge thereby gained, whether as a practitioner in the financial markets, an academic in the field or even as a postgraduate student.

ACKNOWLEDGEMENTS

It would not have been possible to complete this book without the support of the kind people around me, only some of whom is it possible to mention here.

Firstly, I am grateful to Mehrdad Tamiz, Dylan Jones, Carlos Romero and Alejandro Balbas for introducing me to the world of Goal Programming.

Secondly, I would like to acknowledge all the referees and reviewers of my relevant publications for their input and insightful feedback, as well as the valuable informal comments I have received from a wide range of investment experts.

Special gratitude is due to Fadia Abdel Salam, my dear mother and friend, who encouraged me to finish this book amid a major health crisis. I am deeply grateful to her, and to my father and my siblings, for their loving support.

Finally, my thanks go to all the people at Cambridge Scholars Publishing who worked on this book, and to Ben Young of Babel Editing for his careful proofreading. I, of course, retain responsibility for its contents, as well as for any omissions which may unwittingly remain, and will gladly receive comments from readers at rania.a.azmi@gmail.com.

LIST OF ABBREVIATIONS AND NOTATIONS

- APT: Arbitrage Pricing Theory.
- Asset: a financial asset, the term being used throughout this book to indicate either stocks or mutual funds.
- CAPM: Capital Asset Pricing Model.
- GP: Goal Programming.
- LGP: Lexicographic Goal Programming.
- MAD: Mean-Absolute Deviation.
- MF: Mutual Fund.
- PS: Portfolio Selection.
- WGP: Weighted Goal Programming.
- n_i : the ith negative deviational variable.
- α_i : the weighting factor for negative deviational variable *i*.
- p_i : the ith positive deviational variable.
- β_i : the weighting factor for positive deviational variable *i*.
- $\mathbf{x}$: the vector of the decision variables.
- $f_i(\mathbf{x})$: the ith objective function.
- b_i : the ith target value.

- σ_{ij} : the covariance between financial assets *i* and *j*.
- R_j: Return of the jth asset.
- R_f : Risk-free rate.
- λ : Lambda, represents the maximum deviation.
- S_j : Sharpe Ratio for the jth asset, $j = 1, \ldots, n$.
- SD_j : Standard deviation of the jth asset.
- T_j : Treynor Ratio for the jth asset, $j = 1, \ldots, n$.
- $Beta_j$: Beta Coefficient of the jth asset.
- I_t : Return of relevant index (benchmark) during period *t*.
- RS_t : Return of Sharpe's portfolio.
- RT_t : Return of Treynor's portfolio.
- RGP_t : Return of GP's portfolio.
- RBM_t : Return of the relevant benchmark (index).
- TE : the Tracking Error.
- RE : the average return in percentage.
- RI : the total risk as measured by the standard deviation.
- AG : the mutual fund age in years.
- GD : the Gross Domestic Product in Purchasing Power Parity as a percentage of world's total.
- CA : the current account balance as a percentage of the GDP.
- IN : the annual inflation rate in percentage change.

- RG : the regional preferences factor.
- h_q : the qth priority level in an LGP model.

CHAPTER ONE

INTRODUCING GOAL PROGRAMMING FOR REAL-WORLD INVESTMENT DECISION MAKING

Finance theory was instrumental in the growth and development of the financial sector. Available data for the period 1980-2007 in the U.S. show that in 1980 the value of financial assets was slightly above that of U.S. GDP (129% of GDP including derivatives). In 1990, the value of the financial assets was more than twice that of GDP (253%). By 2001, the value of the stock of global financial assets was almost six times that of world GDP and by 2007 it represented thirteen times the value of world GDP (Caldentey and Vernengo, 2010).

The investment methods used to reach the desired objectives range from quantitative investment, which originated in modern portfolio theory, to more traditional methods of financial analysis. Quantitative investment techniques are now among the most widely used fund management methods. They are generally grouped into two major categories: active investment management and passive investment management. Passive investment covers index investment. The objective of active investment management is to perform better than the market, or better than a benchmark that is chosen as a reference (Grinold and Kahn, 1995).

The basic elements that allow portfolios to be created are assets. These assets, which are traded on financial markets, are numerous and vary greatly in nature. The simplest way to group assets together is to consider asset classes, such as stocks, bonds, etc. Each asset class corresponds to a level of risk (Amenc and Le Sourd, 2003).

For the applications and experiments carried out in this book assets are considered to be either stocks or mutual funds. Stocks represent shares of ownership in a company, while mutual funds are investment companies that create a large pool of money that can be invested in stocks, bonds or other securities. Bonds are the most common lending investment traded on securities markets (Tyson, 2007).

Mutual funds have become a popular structure for investors seeking exposure to financial markets. Gregoriou (2007) claims there are two reasons why rational investors delegate their wealth management to mutual funds: first, economies of scale which reduce wealth management costs; second, private investors might expect that professional mutual fund managers have superior management skills, leading to positive risk-adjusted excess returns.

A portfolio is defined as a grouping of assets. An investor can invest in a portfolio of stocks or a portfolio of mutual funds. Portfolio management is about risk and return—although good returns are difficult to achieve and good risk-adjusted returns can be difficult to identify. The concept of return requires no explanation other than to comment that larger returns are preferred to smaller ones. Risk is more challenging, and is inherently a probabilistic or statistical concept. There are various, and sometimes conflicting, notions and measures of risk. As a result, it can be difficult to measure the risk of a portfolio and determine how various investments and asset allocations affect that risk (Pearson, 2002; Travers, 2004).

Risk means different things to different market participants. For theory building, it is important that risk be defined in terms of rational investors, and it is desirable that there is a consensus among all rational investors as to what constitutes risk (Markowitz, 1995). To an investor, the risk of a historical portfolio is the uncertainty or degree of dispersion in the probability distribution of its future market value (Hymans and Mulligan, 1980).

To be able to make decisions, it must be possible to quantify the degree of risk in a particular opportunity. The most common method is to use the standard deviation of the expected returns. This method measures spreads, and it is the possible returns of these spreads that provide the measure of risk. However, there are several different factors that cause risk or lead to variability in returns on an individual investment. Factors that may influence risk in any given investment vehicle include uncertainty of income, interest rates, inflation, exchange rates, the state of the economy, liquidity risk, etc. The goal is to hold a group of investments within a portfolio potentially to reduce the risk level suffered without reducing the level of return (Pearson, 2002).

An important insight of modern financial theory is that some investment risks yield an expected reward, while other risks do not. Risks that can be eliminated by diversification (called unsystematic risks) do not yield an expected reward, while risks that cannot be eliminated by diversification (called systematic or market risks) do yield an expected reward. Diversification reduces risk, but only up to a point (Corrado and Jordan, 2005) as illustrated in figure 1.1.

Figure 1.1: Diversifiable and Non-Diversifiable Risks

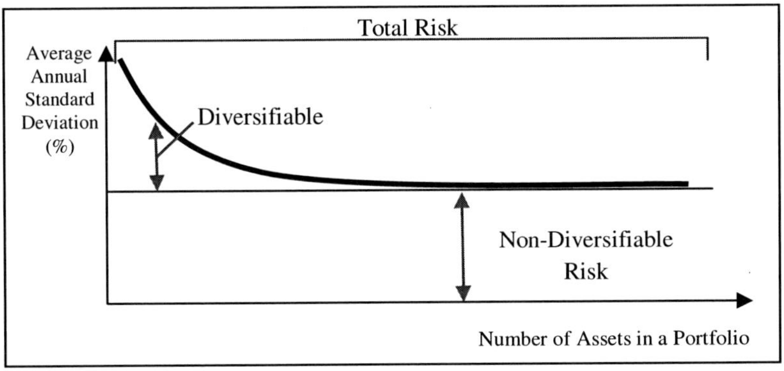

In portfolio management it is common to think about risk in terms of a portfolio's return relative to the return on a benchmark portfolio. Market indices are quoted on stock exchanges and are therefore simple to use as benchmarks. In particular, if the FTSE 100 index is the benchmark, an investor might be concerned about the difference between the return on his/her portfolio and the return on the FTSE 100, rather than on the return on the portfolio only.

Portfolio Selection issues have been the subject of extensive research ever since Markowitz's pioneer article on the topic (1952). In an autobiography written at the time of his Nobel Prize in 1990, Markowitz mentioned that the focus in much research has been on the application of mathematical or computer techniques to practical problems, in which existing techniques were applied or new techniques were developed (Frangsmyr, 1991).

Markowitz (1991) was the first to quantify the link that exists between portfolio risk and portfolio return. By this, he founded modern portfolio theory. The Markowitz model was the starting point for numerous developments in finance. It contains, in particular, the fundamental elements of the Capital Asset Pricing Model which is the source of the first risk-adjusted performance measures (Sharpe, 1963; 1964; Treynor, 1965).

The Markowitz theory (1952) does not speak of efficient markets, but of efficient portfolios. The market is efficient if the prices of assets at any moment reflect all available information (Amenc and Le Sourd, 2003). An efficient portfolio is defined as a portfolio with minimal risk for a given return, or, equivalently, as the portfolio with the highest return for a given level of risk.

To construct a portfolio, investors need to define first the categories of assets that they wish to include in the portfolio, depending on their objectives and constraints. The asset allocation methods may depend on the nature of the assets, but, in all cases, asset allocation is carried out in two stages:

- Investors define the long-term allocation, based on the risk and return estimations for each asset class. This is strategic allocation.
- Investors may carry out adjustments based on short-term anticipations. This is tactical allocation.

The last stage in the construction of a portfolio is the stock picking, or more generally, assets picking. This takes into account the microeconomic market trends and concerns stocks in particular. In addition to the methods drawn from modern portfolio theory, some methods allow stock picking to be carried out on a quantitative basis. Once the portfolio has been constructed, the final stage of the investment management process consists of evaluating its performance (Amenc and Le Sourd, 2003).

Managing the portfolio is an integral part of portfolio construction, wherein an investor seeks to regularly readjust the proportions of the different asset classes in the portfolio, to take into account short-term forecasts of market movements and the evolution of the economic environment, while respecting the risk constraints. Therefore, a portfolio cannot be analysed as a closed system without some consideration of the responsiveness of assets to external factors and asset-specific performance (Lee, 1972).

While emphasising the importance of selecting suitable factors for portfolio analysis, Markowitz (1995) designs his model based on only two objectives, as they are the common ones to all investors.

Elton and Gruber (1995) discuss the two categories for breakthroughs in implementation of portfolio theory in the following terms:

- Simplifications of the amount and type of input data needed to perform portfolio analysis.
- Simplification of the computational procedure needed to calculate optimal portfolios.

A great deal of research by academics and financial practitioners has been devoted to performance measurement for portfolios (allowing past results to be quantified) and performance analysis (allowing the results to be explained).

As has often been noted (Lee, 1972; Lai and Hwang, 1994), a major concern in making decisions is that almost all decision problems have multiple and usually conflicting criteria. The soundness of decision making is thus measured by the degree to which the relevant goals are achieved. To that end, an application of the scientific approach is necessary, and this calls for systematic analysis of the decision system. Systematic investigation enables the decision maker to consider all pertinent factors related to the decision so that the best ultimate course of action can be identified from among a set of alternatives.

The book strives to provide both practitioners and academics with a scientific approach to portfolio selection using goal programming, an approach which is capable as far as is possible of achieving a required set of preferences.

Goal Programming (GP) is perhaps the most widely used approach in the field of multiple criteria decision making that enables the decision maker to incorporate numerous variations of constraints and goals. The original portfolio selection problem, with risk and return optimisation, can be viewed as a case of Goal Programming with two objectives. Additional objectives representing other factors can be introduced for a more realistic approach to portfolio selection problems.

Although any Goal Programming problem of meaningful size would be solved on the computers, the notion of programming in GP is associated with the development of solutions, or programs, for a specific problem. Hence, GP has nothing intrinsically to do with computer programming and the name GP is used to indicate seeking the (optimal) program for a mathematical model that is composed solely of goals (Ignizio, 1985).

Ignizio and Romero (2003) highlight that real-world decision problems are usually changeable, complex and resist treatment with conventional approaches. Therefore, the optimisation of a single objective subject to a set of rigid constraints is in most cases unrealistic, and that is why Goal Programming was introduced, in an attempt to eliminate or at least mitigate this shortcoming.

The two philosophical concepts that serve to best distinguish Goal Programming from conventional methods of optimisation (with a single objective) are the incorporation of flexibility in constraint functions and the adherence to the philosophy of Satisficing as opposed to Optimisation.

Satisficing is an old Scots word that refers to the desire to find a practical and real-world solution to a problem, rather than an idealistic or optimal solution to a highly simplified model of that problem. In Goal Programming, the decision maker usually seeks a useful, practical, implementable and attainable solution rather than one satisfying the mathematician's desire.

CHAPTER TWO

SELECTED LITERATURE ON GOAL PROGRAMMING FOR INVESTMENT DECISION MAKING AND MODELLING

2.1 Introduction to Goal Programming for Portfolio Selection

Finance theory has produced a variety of models that attempt to provide some insight into the environment in which financial decisions are made. By definition, every model is a simplification of reality. Hence, even if the data fail to reject the model, the decision maker may not necessarily want to place too much weight on it. At the same time, the notion that the models implied by finance theory could be entirely worthless seems rather extreme. Hence, even if the data reject the model, the decision maker may still want to use the model at least to some degree (Pastor, 2000).

Some researchers involved in the mean-variance analysis of Markowitz (1952) for portfolio selection have only focused on PS as risk-adjusted return with little or no effort being directed to the inclusion of other essential factors. Therefore, the usual portfolio analysis assumes that investors are interested only in returns attached to specific levels of risk when selecting their portfolios. In a wide variety of applications, neither part of this restriction is desirable or important. Consequently, a portfolio analysis model that includes more factors in the analysis of portfolio problems is a more realistic approach. Some of these factors include asset region, micro economics, macro economics, liquidity and market dynamics.

The purpose of the analysis of portfolio is to find portfolios which best meet the objectives of the investor. A portfolio analysis must be based on criteria which serve as a guide to the important and unimportant, the relevant and irrelevant (Markowitz, 1995).

As mentioned in the previous chapter, the original portfolio selection problems, which are concerned with risk and return optimisation, can be viewed as a case of Goal Programming with two objectives. Additional objectives representing other factors can be introduced for a more realistic approach to PS problems.

Charnes, Cooper and Ferguson developed Goal Programming in 1955. GP is a multi-objective programming technique. The ethos of GP lies in the Simonian concept of satisficing of objectives (Tamiz, Jones and Romero, 1998). Herbert Simon introduced the concept of satisficing in 1956, a word that originated in Northumbria, in the Scottish border regions, where it meant "to satisfy." Satisficing is a strategy for making decisions in cases wherein one has to choose among various alternatives which are encountered sequentially, and which are not known ahead of time (Ignizio and Romero, 2003; Reina, 2005).

GP is an important technique for decision-making problems where the decision maker aims to minimise the deviation between the achievement of goals and their aspiration levels. It can be said that GP has been, and still is, the most widely used multi-objective technique in management science because of its inherent flexibility in handling decision-making problems with several conflicting objectives and incomplete or imprecise information (Romero, 1991, 2004; Chang, 2007).

Ignizio and Romero (2003) label Goal Programming as the workhorse of multiple objective optimisation, as over many years GP has seen successful solutions for important real-world problems, such as the following:

- The analysis of executive compensation for General Electric.
- The design and deployment of the antenna for the Saturn II launch vehicle as employed in the Apollo manned moon-landing program.
- The determination of a siting scheme for the Patriot Air Defence System.
- The design of acoustic arrays for U.S. Navy torpedoes.
- The audit transactions within the financial sector and a host of problems in the area of finance, resource allocation, etc.

2.2 The Use of Multi-Criteria Decision Analysis in Portfolio Selection and the Importance of Goal Programming

Optimisation is a process by which the most favourable trade-off between competing interests is determined subject to the constraints faced in any decision-making process. Within the context of portfolio management, the competing interests are, among others, risk reduction and return enhancement (Kritzman, 2003).

Present-day theory of portfolio analysis prescribes a way of thinking about opportunities for investment. Instead of extensive evaluation of a single asset in isolation, the theory prescribes that investment policy be formulated in a manner in which a purchase of an asset is done if and only if it will cause a rise in the overall personal satisfactions. A rise may come about via one of three schemes as follows (Renwick, 1969):

- The new asset can cause a net increase in total present expected return on the portfolio.
- The new asset can cause a net decline in total risk exposure on the entire portfolio.
- There can be some subjectively acceptable trade off between change in total risk and change in total expected return on the portfolio.

The first two are the traditional and direct schemes for selecting portfolios, while the third is open to many possibilities and consequently has stimulated many studies in search of better portfolio selection strategies for investors.

Besides portfolio selection issues, there is the issue of performance measurement for portfolios. Treynor (1965), Sharpe (1966) and Jensen (1968) develop the standard indices to measure portfolios' performances, i.e., risk-adjusted returns for portfolios.

Numerous studies have tested the performance of portfolios (mutual funds) compared to a certain benchmark, usually a market index, based on Sharpe, Treynor and Jensen's performance measures (Artikis, 2002; Cresson, Cudd and Lipscomb, 2002; Daniel et al., 1997; Lehmann and Modest, 1987; Matallin and Nieto, 2002; Otten and Schweitzer, 2002; Raj, Forsyth and Tomini, 2003; Zheng, 1999).

Bottom-line performance measurement concentrates on the question of how a portfolio fared, both absolutely and relative to a benchmark.

Markowitz (1952) suggests that investors should consider risk and return together and determine the allocation of funds among investment alternatives on the basis of the trade-off between them. Later, the recognition that many investors evaluate performance relative to a benchmark led to the idea of PS based on return and relative risk (Cremers, Kritzman and Page, 2005). For many investors, both approaches fail to yield satisfactory results. Chow (1995) emphasises that portfolio optimisation techniques can assist in the search for the portfolio that best suits each investor's particular objectives.

An alternative to the Markowitz model is the Mean-Absolute Deviation (MAD) model, proposed by Konno and Yamazaki (1991). While the

Markowitz model assumes the normality of stock returns, the MAD model does not make this assumption. The MAD model also minimises a measure of risk, where the measure is the mean absolute deviation (Kim, Kim and Shin, 2005; Konno and Koshizuka, 2005). Konno and Yamazaki (1991) further develop the MAD model into an equivalent GP model.

Konno and Kobayashi (1997) propose a new model for constructing an integrated stock-bond portfolio, which serves as an alternative to the popular asset allocation strategy. The fund is first allocated to indexes corresponding to diverse asset classes and then allocated to individual assets using appropriate models for each asset class.

Their model (Konno and Kobayashi, 1997) determines the allocation of the fund to individual assets in one stage by solving a large scale mean-variance or mean-absolute deviation model using newly developed technologies in large-scale quadratic programming and linear programming analysis, respectively. Computational experiments show that the new approach can serve as a more reliable and less expensive method to allocate the fund to diverse classes of assets.

Konno (2003) shows that there is a possibility of applying standard portfolio optimisation methods to the management of small- and medium-scale funds. Konno (2003) shows that the use of the mean-absolute deviation model can handle concave transaction costs and minimal transaction unit constraints in an efficient manner using a branch and bound algorithm. But the transaction cost is still not negligible for the majority of standard investors.

Parra, Terol and Uria (2001), amongst other authors, claim that there has been a growing interest in incorporating additional criteria beyond risk and return into the PS process. Multiple criteria PS problems normally stem from multiple-argument investor utility functions. For investors with additional concerns, steps can be taken to integrate them into the portfolio optimisation process more in accordance with their criteria status.

Chow (1995) mentions that investment practitioners have implicitly sent a message that optimisation models have limited relevance in real-world investment decisions. One of the best arguments for this assertion is that few investors allocate their assets in the proportions indicated by an optimisation model.

Furthermore, Christiansen and Vames (2008) present a framework for understanding how portfolio decision making is shaped through appropriate decision making. They find that the identity of the decision maker is shaped and influenced by four factors: the formal system and rules, observations of others, the organisational context, and organisational learning. In practice, the decision maker must deal with multiple factors and criteria that make it difficult to carry out a traditional rational decision-making process.

In addition, Rifai (1996) highlights the fact that the survival of any U.S. firm in the national and international markets depends on the use of scientific techniques in their decision-making processes. The utilisation of scientific techniques requires certain steps to be followed. The most important steps are identifying, quantifying and solving the problem. He describes GP as a very powerful quantitative model, which, if used properly, can be an excellent tool, particularly for investment decisions.

Cremers et al. (2005) emphasise the importance of using more approaches to portfolio formulation, particularly mean-variance optimisation and full-scale optimisation approaches. Cremers et al. (2005) argue that institutional investors typically use mean-variance optimisation in PS, in part because it requires knowledge of only the expected returns, standard deviations, and correlations of the portfolio's components, while other investors prefer to use full-scale optimisation as an alternative to mean-variance optimisation since computational advances now facilitate performing such full-scale optimisations. Under this approach, the PS process considers as many asset mixes as necessary in order to identify the proportions that yield the highest expected utility, given any utility function.

Renwick (1969) mentions that investment portfolio behaviour can be characterised and classified using combinations of four interrelated variables: rate of return on total assets, rate of growth of output, capital structure, and rate of retention of available income.

The evidence which Renwick presents in his paper (1969) supports the view that dividend policy is relevant to the investment decision as well as that finance does matter for the valuation of corporate assets. Current and anticipated future returns on investment, along with the various types of risks associated with those returns, all interact to determine and characterise the empirical behaviour and performance of investor portfolios.

Despite the volume of research supporting standard PS, there has always been a slight undercurrent of multiple objectives in PS, but this is changing.

Generally, in PS problems the decision maker simultaneously considers conflicting objectives such as rate of return, risk and liquidity. Multi-objective programming techniques, such as GP, are used to choose the portfolio best satisfying the decision maker's aspirations and preferences.

The following figure illustrates the rise in the number of publications of research papers in the area of PS using GP:

Figure 2.1: The development in the number of publications on Goal Programming for Portfolio Selection

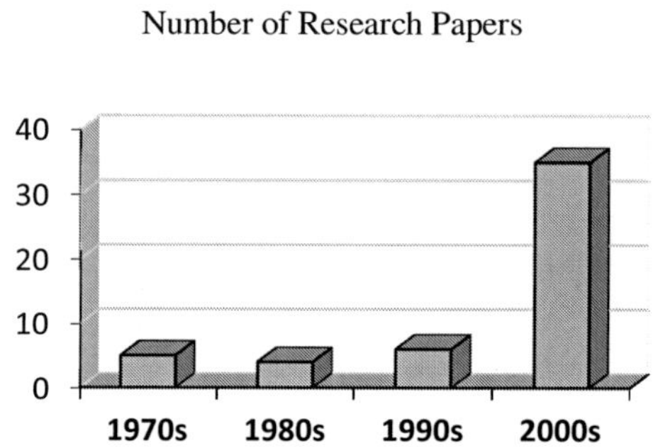

Significant advances have taken place in recent years in the field of GP. A higher level of computerised automation of the solution and modelling process has brought use of the already existing and new analysis techniques within reach of the average practitioner (Tamiz and Jones, 1998).

2.3 Portfolio Selection Using Goal Programming: Theoretical and Practical Developments

The ultimate objective of optimal Portfolio Selection (PS) is to determine and hold a portfolio which offers the minimum possible deviation for a given or desired expected return. But this objective assumes a stable financial environment. In a world in which an investor is certain of the future, the optimal PS problem is reduced to that of structuring a portfolio that will maximise the investor's return.

Unfortunately, the future is not certain, and particularly now as never before; consequently the solution to the optimal PS problem will depend upon the following elements (Callin, 2008):

- A set of possible future scenarios for the world.
- A correspondence function, linking possible future scenarios to the returns of individual securities.
- A probabilities function of the likelihood of each of the possible future scenarios of the world.
- A way to determine whether one portfolio is preferable to another portfolio.

These elements are considered under different assumptions based on investors' strategies, and their analysis is achievable through the GP approach.

Kumar, Philippatos and Ezzell (1978) highlight the fact that standard PS techniques are typically characterised by motivational assumptions of unified goals or objectives. Therefore, their immediate relevance to real-world situations, usually marked by the presence of several conflicting goals, is at best limited.

Nevertheless, with appropriate extensions the standard techniques can form the basis for accommodating multiple goals. Kumar et al. (1978) address the problem of goal conflicts in the PS of Dual-Purpose Funds, and suggest an extension of standard methodology, in terms of the development of a GP model in conceptual form, which can be applied for the resolution of inherent clash of interests.

GP in PS context is an analytical approach devised to address financial decision-making problems where targets have been assigned to the attributes of a portfolio and where the decision maker is interested in minimising the non-achievement of the corresponding goals.

During recent years many models concerning PS using GP have been developed. Amongst the research papers that introduce such models are the ones shown in the following table (table 2.1).

Romero (2004) claims that most GP applications reported in the literature use a weighted or lexicographic achievement function. Romero explains that this selection is usually made in a rather mechanistic way without theoretical justification, and that if the selection of the achievement function is wrong, then it is very likely that the decision maker will not accept the solution. The majority of research papers prior to 2000 develop PS models utilising weighted and/or lexicographic GP variants. This trend has since changed to the fuzzy goal programming variant, and most recently into the main variants of weighted, lexicographic and MinMax GP variants. When attributes and/or goals are in an imprecise environment and cannot be stated with precision, it is appropriate to use fuzzy GP. A primary challenge in today's financial world is to determine how to proceed in the face of uncertainty, which arises from incomplete data and from imperfect knowledge. Volatility is an important challenge too, since estimates of volatility allow us to assess the likelihood of experiencing a particular outcome.

Table 2.1: Research papers on GP for PS since 1970s to present

Year	Author	Portfolio Selection Using Goal Programming
1973	Lee & Lerro	LGP (PS for Mutual Funds)
1975	Stone & Reback	Other Variant (Nonlinear GP)
1977	Booth & Dash	Other Variant (Nonlinear GP- Bank Portfolio)
1978	Kumar, Philippatos & Ezzell	LGP (Dual-Purpose Funds)
	Muhlemann, Lockett & Gear	LGP (Portfolio Modelling)
1979	Kumar & Philippatos	LGP (Dual-Purpose Funds)
1980	Lee & Chesser	LGP (PS)
1984	Levary & Avery	LGP (Weighting Equities in a Portfolio)
1985	Alexander & Resnich	LGP (Bond Portfolios)
1991	Konno & Yamazaki	MAD, PS
1994	Byrne & Lee	Spreadsheet Optimizer (RE Portfolio)
1996	Tamiz, Hasham & Jones	Two Staged GP Model for Portfolio Selection
1997	Tamiz, Hasham, Fargher & Jones	Comparison between GP and regression analysis for PS
	Watada	Fuzzy Portfolio Selection
1998	Kooros & McManis	Multiattribute Optimisation for Strategic Investment Decisions
2000	Deng, Wang & Xia	Criteria, Models & Strategies in PS
	Inuiguchi & Ramik	Fuzzy GP and Other Variant
	Ogryczak	Linear Programming Model for PS
2001	Jobst, Horniman, Lucas & Mitra	Other Variant (Alternative Portfolio Selection Models)
	Parra, Terol & Uria	FGP (Portfolio Selection)
2002	Wang & Zhu	Fuzzy Portfolio Selection
	Zopounidis & Doumpos	Multi-criteria Decision Aid in Financial DM
2003	Allen, Bhattacharya & Smarandache	Other Variant- Portfolio Optimisation
	Prakash, Chang & Pactwa	Other Variant- Polynomial GP (Selecting Portfolio with Skewness)
	Rostamy, Azar & Hosseini	Other Variant
	Sun & Yan	Other Variant- Skewness & Optimal PS
2004	Kosmidou & Zopounidis	GP, Simulation Analysis & Bank Asset Liability Management
	Pendaraki, Doumpos & Zopounidis	GP (Equity Mutual Fund Portfolios)
2005	Dash & Kajiji	Other Variant (Nonlinear GP for Asset-Liability Management)
	Davies, Kat & Lu	Other Variant (Polynomial GP- Fund of Hedge Funds PS)
	Deng, Li & Wang	Minimax Portfolio Selection
	Pendaraki, Zopounidis & Doumpos	GP- Construction of Mutual Funds Portfolios

	Tektas, Ozkan-Gunay & Gunay	GP- Asset & Liability Management
2006	Bilbao et al.	GP- Portfolio Selection with Expert Betas
	Sharma & Sharma	LGP for Mutual Funds
2007	Abdelaziz, Aouni & ElFayedh	Other Variant
	Bilbao, Arenas, Rodriguez & Antomil	Goal Programming
	Gladish, Jones, Tamiz & Terol	Interactive Three-Stage Model- Mutual Funds Portfolio Selection
	Li & Xu	Other Variant (Nonlinear GP- PS)
	Sharma, Ghosh & Sharma	Other Variant (Credit Union Portfolio Management)
	Wu, Chou, Yang & Ong	GP- Index Investing
2008	Huang	Fuzzy GP for PS
2009	Fulga	Multistage Portfolio Optimisation
2010	Garcia, Guijarro & Moya	GP for estimating performance weights
2010	Azmi & Tamiz	Review of GP for Portfolio Selection
2010	Tamiz & Azmi	Mutual Funds PS for Emerging Market
2011	Azmi	Investment Portfolio Selection using GP
2011	Tamiz, Azmi & Jones	Selecting Portfolios based on Sharpe, Treynor and Goal Programming Methodologies
2013	Tamiz, Azmi & Jones	On selecting portfolio of international MFs using GP with extended factors.

2.4 The Main Goal Programming Variants for Portfolio Selection

Romero (2004) mentions that a key element of a GP model is the achievement function, which measures the degree of minimisation of the unwanted deviational variables of the model's goals. Different types of achievement functions lead to different GP variants as follows.

2.4.1 Weighted Goal Programming in Portfolio Selection Models

The weighted GP for PS model usually lists the unwanted deviational variables, each weighted according to their importance.

Weighted Goal Programming (WGP) attaches weights according to the relative importance of each objective as perceived by the decision maker and minimises the sum of the unwanted weighted deviations (Tamiz and Jones, 1995). For example, the objective function in a WGP model for PS seeks to minimise risk and maximise return by penalising excess risk and shortfalls in return, relative to the respective targets. Therefore, lower levels of risk and higher levels of return are not penalised. Additional objectives specifying other portfolio attributes, such as liquidity, cost of rebalancing and regional allocation, can be included in the WGP model.

2.4.2 Lexicographic Goal Programming in Portfolio Selection Models

The achievement function of the Lexicographic Goal Programming (LGP) model for PS is made up of an ordered vector whose dimension coincides with the q number of priority levels established in the model. Each component in this vector represents the unwanted deviational variables of the goals placed in the corresponding priority level.

Lexicographic achievement functions imply a non-compensatory structure of preferences. In other words, there are no finite trade-offs among goals placed in different priority levels (Romero, 2004).

The priority structure for the model can be established by assigning each goal or a set of goals to a priority level, thereby ranking the goals lexicographically in order of importance to the decision maker. When achieving one goal is equally important as achieving other goals, such as the goals of risk and return, then they may be included at the same priority level, where numerical weights represent the relative importance of the goals at the same priority level (Sharma and Sharma, 2006).

LGP could thus deal with many priority levels in a PS problem in which goal constraints are included according to their importance of achievement in the model. For example, a PS model using LGP may include the following priority structure:

1. Maximising the portfolio's expected return, while minimising some measurement of portfolio risk.
2. Minimising other portfolio risks (e.g., the systematic risk as measured by the Beta Coefficient).
3. Minimising the portfolio's cost of rebalancing.
+ Other priority levels.

Many authors have developed lexicographic GP models for PS, particularly during the 1970s and 1980s (for example, Lee and Lerro, 1973; Kumar, Philippatos and Ezzell, 1978; Levary and Avery, 1984). Other applications of LGP for PS include the mutual funds industry (Sharma and Sharma, 2006).

2.4.3 MinMax Goal Programming in Portfolio Selection Models

The achievement function of a MinMax (Chebyshev) GP model implies the minimisation of the maximum deviation from any single goal. Moreover, when some conditions hold the corresponding solution represents a balanced allocation among the achievement of the different goals (Romero, 1991).

The model of MinMax (Chebyshev) GP portfolio selection usually seeks the minimisation of the maximum deviation from any single goal in PS. In other words, it seeks the solution that minimises the worst unwanted deviation from any single goal.

Some authors focus historically on developing PS models using the MinMax GP variant. Deng, Li and Wang (2005), amongst others, develop a MinMax GP model for PS.

2.4.4 Other Goal Programming Variants in Portfolio Selection Models

While the weighted, lexicographic and MinMax forms of the achievement function are the most widely used, other recently developed variants may represent the decision makers' preferences or decision-making circumstances in some cases, most notably fuzzy GP.

Fuzzy mathematical programming has been developed for treating uncertainties in the setting of optimisation problems. This fuzzy mathematical programming can be classified into three categories with respect to the kind of uncertainties treated in the method (Inuiguchi and Ramik, 2000):

- Fuzzy mathematical programming with vagueness.
- Fuzzy mathematical programming with ambiguity.
- Fuzzy mathematical programming with combined vagueness and ambiguity.

Vagueness is associated with the difficulty of making sharp or precise distinctions in the world; that is, some domain of interest is vague if it cannot be delimited by sharp boundaries. Ambiguity is associated with one-to-many relations, that is, situations in which the choice between two or more alternatives is left unspecified (Inuiguchi & Ramik, 2000).

In fuzzy GP portfolio selection model, the decision maker is required to specify an aspiration level for each objective in the model in which aspiration levels are not known precisely. In this case, an objective with an imprecise level can be treated as a fuzzy goal (Yaghoobi and Tamiz, 2006).

The use of fuzzy models not only avoids unrealistic modelling but also offers a chance for reducing information costs. Fuzzy sets are used in fuzzy mathematical programming both to define the objective and constraints and also to reflect the aspiration levels given by the decision makers (Leon, Liern and Vercher, 2002).

In this context, Watada (1997) argues that the Markowitz approach to PS has difficulty in resolving situations in which the aspiration level and utility given by the decision makers cannot be defined exactly. Watada (1997) therefore proposes a fuzzy PS to overcome this difficulty. The fuzzy PS enables one to obtain the best solution which can be realised given a vague aspiration level and where the goal is given as a fuzzy number, in view of the expertise of the decision makers.

Gladish et al. (2007) argue that the PS problem is characterised by the imprecision and/or vagueness inherent in the required data, and propose a three-stage model in order to mitigate such problems, based on a multi-index model and considering several market scenarios described in an imprecise way by an expert.

Leon et al. (2002) focus on the infeasible instances of different models which are suppose to select the best portfolio according to their respective objective functions. They propose an algorithm to repair the infeasibility. Such infeasibility, which is usually provoked by the conflict between the desired return and the diversification requirements proposed by the investor, could be avoided by using fuzzy linear programming techniques.

Parra, Terol and Uria (2001) deal with the optimum portfolio for a private investor with emphasis on three criteria: expected return of the portfolio, the variance return of the portfolio, and the portfolio's liquidity measured as the possibility of converting an investment into cash without any significant loss in value. Parra et al. (2001) formulate these three objectives as a GP problem using fuzzy terms since they cannot be defined exactly from the point of view of the investors. Parra et al. propose a method to determine portfolios with fuzzy attributes that are set equal to fuzzy target values. Their solution is based on the investor's preferences and on the GP techniques.

Allen, Bhattacharya and Smarandache (2003) investigate the notion of fuzziness with respect to funds allocation. They find that the boundary between the preference sets of an individual investor, for funds allocations between a risk-free asset and the risky market portfolio, tends to be rather fuzzy, as the investors continually evaluate and shift their positions; unless, that is, it is a passive buy-and-hold kind of portfolio.

Inuiguchi and Ramik (2000) emphasise that the real-world problems are not usually so easily formulated as mathematical models or fuzzy models. Sometimes qualitative constraints and/or objectives are almost impossible to represent in mathematical forms. Inuiguchi and Ramik (2000) apply fuzzy mathematical programming in PS problems and find that the decision maker can only select the final solution from the fuzzy solution by considering implicit and mathematically weak requirements.

2.5 Conclusion

Goal Programming for Portfolio Selection problems has been deployed extensively over recent decades. This chapter has briefly reviewed many of the highlights. GP models for PS allow the incorporation of multiple goals such as portfolio return, risk, regional preferences, and other factors. There is a huge capacity for future developments and applications of GP for PS issues. In particular, GP could be used for incorporating extended factors into the PS analysis and obtaining its constituents' proportions.

CHAPTER THREE

KEY METHODOLOGIES FOR INVESTMENT PORTFOLIO SELECTION

3.1 Introduction

In order to provide a meaningful comparison and analysis of portfolio selection output, this book uses other methods besides Goal Programming for Portfolio Selection. These methods are Markowitz, Konno's model, Sharpe and Treynor.

Two sets of consecutive returns within distinguishable time periods are used in the various chapters of this book. These time periods are the "constructing" period, used for setting up portfolios, and the "testing" period, used for measuring their performance.

A spreadsheet (Microsoft Office Excel) and its Solver are used to model and solve the problem of portfolio selection of assets. Different weighting algorithms are applied in order to finalise constructing portfolios and to test their performances.

The term "asset" in this book stands for a financial asset, used throughout to indicate either stocks or mutual funds. However, a financial asset is broadly defined as a financial claim on an asset that is usually documented by some type of legal representation. Examples include shares of stock, but not tangible assets such as real estate or gold.

3.2 Markowitz

3.2.1 The Model

The first mathematical model for portfolio selection was formed by Markowitz (1952). In the Markowitz portfolio selection model, the return on a portfolio is measured by the expected value of the portfolio return, while the associated risk is measured by the variance of the portfolio return.

Markowitz showed that the risk of an asset that really matters is not the risk of each asset in isolation but the contribution that each asset makes to the risk of the aggregate portfolio. With this insight Markowitz reduced the complicated and multidimensional problem of portfolio construction with respect to a large number of different assets, all with varying properties, to a conceptually simple two-dimensional problem known as "mean-variance" analysis (Teresiene and Paskevicius, 2009).

The Markowitz model, or the Mean-Variance model, is as follows:

$$Min \sum_{i=1}^{n} \sum_{j=1}^{n} x_i \sigma_{ij} x_j$$

Subject to:

$$\sum_{j=1}^{n} R_j X_j \geq D$$

$$\sum_{j=1}^{n} X_j = 1 \qquad (3.1)$$

$$X_j \geq 0 \qquad j = 1, \dots, n$$

Where:

σ_{ij}= The covariance between financial assets *i* and *j*.

x_i= The proportion invested in asset *i*.

x_j= The proportion invested in asset *j*.

n= The number of assets in the portfolio.

R_j= Return of the jth asset.

D = The desired level of return.

Constraint (3.1) is introduced to ensure the usage of the entire fund.

3.2.2 The Model in the Spreadsheet

The standard spreadsheet Solver (Microsoft Office Excel Solver) is used to find the optimal solution (solution that satisfies the constraints set above and minimises the objective function). An optimisation model has three parts: the target cell, the changing cells, and the constraints. The Solver uses the terminologies of Target Cell for the objective function value, and Changing Cells for the value of the decision variables. The user can control several options and tolerances through the Solver Option dialogue box.

The Microsoft Office Excel Solver tool uses the algorithms and methods of Generalized Reduced Gradient (GRG2) nonlinear optimisation code for nonlinear problems (Lasdon et al., 1976). Linear and integer programming problems are solved with the Simplex method, with bounds on the variables (Nelder and Mead, 1965), and the branch-and-bound method (Lawler and Wood, 1966) respectively (Winston, 2007).

The following are the key steps for solving the Markowitz model using the spreadsheet:

Step 1: Prepare the data sheet required for Markowitz model, including the covariance matrix as shown in the following figure.

Figure 3.1: The data sheet for the Markowitz model, including the covariance matrix between 5 assets using their return data over a given period of time

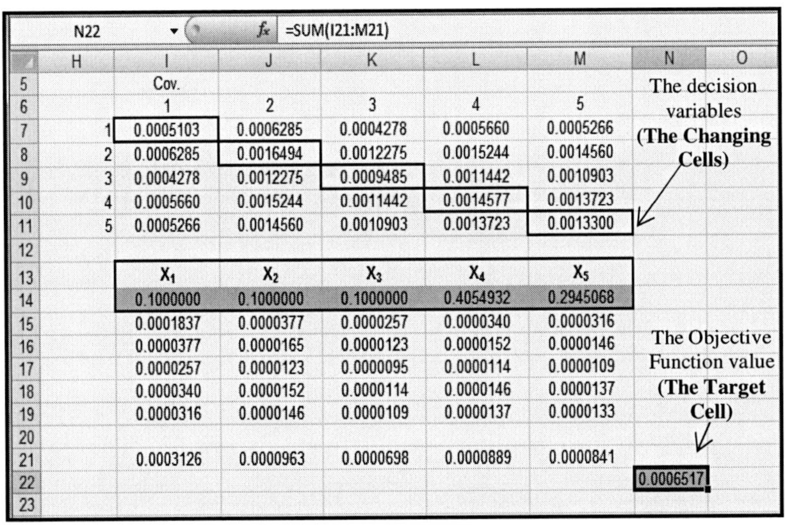

N22 =SUM(I21:M21)

	H	I	J	K	L	M	N	O
5		Cov.						
6		1	2	3	4	5		
7	1	0.0005103	0.0006285	0.0004278	0.0005660	0.0005266		
8	2	0.0006285	0.0016494	0.0012275	0.0015244	0.0014560		
9	3	0.0004278	0.0012275	0.0009485	0.0011442	0.0010903		
10	4	0.0005660	0.0015244	0.0011442	0.0014577	0.0013723		
11	5	0.0005266	0.0014560	0.0010903	0.0013723	0.0013300		
12								
13		X_1	X_2	X_3	X_4	X_5		
14		0.1000000	0.1000000	0.1000000	0.4054932	0.2945068		
15		0.0001837	0.0000377	0.0000257	0.0000340	0.0000316		
16		0.0000377	0.0000165	0.0000123	0.0000152	0.0000146		
17		0.0000257	0.0000123	0.0000095	0.0000114	0.0000109		
18		0.0000340	0.0000152	0.0000114	0.0000146	0.0000137		
19		0.0000316	0.0000146	0.0000109	0.0000137	0.0000133		
20								
21		0.0003126	0.0000963	0.0000698	0.0000889	0.0000841		
22							0.0006517	
23								

The numbers shown in figure 3.1 are calculated using the decision variables (x_j) and the covariance matrix (σ_{ij}) between the assets. The cells from I7 to M11 represent the covariance matrix. The decision variables are in cells I14 to M14. Cells from I15 through M19 represent the corresponding ($x_i \sigma_{ij} x_j$).

For example, cell I15 = $x_1 \sigma_{11} x_1$, while cell I16 = $x_1 \sigma_{12} x_2$. Finally, the objective function value appears in cell N22 which represents $\sum_{i=1}^{n} \sum_{j=1}^{n} x_i \sigma_{ij} x_j$.

Step 2: On the Data tab of the Excel file, in the Analysis group, click Solver in order to fill the Solver parameters corresponding to the model to be solved (in this section it is the Markowitz model) as illustrated in the following table.

Table 3.1: Markowitz model in the spreadsheet

Excel Solver's Parameters	Mathematical representation of Markowitz model	Graphical illustration of spreadsheet usage
Set Target Cell (The objective function value to be minimised)	$Min \sum_{i=1}^{n} \sum_{j=1}^{n} x_i \sigma_{ij} x_j$	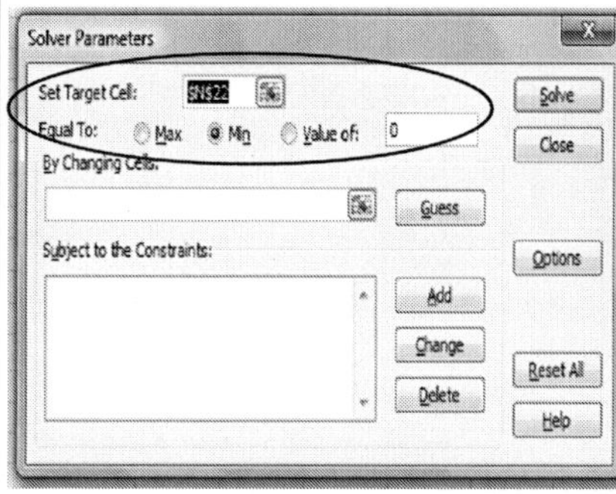

<table>
<tr>
<td>By Changing Cells</td>
<td>x_i and x_j</td>
<td>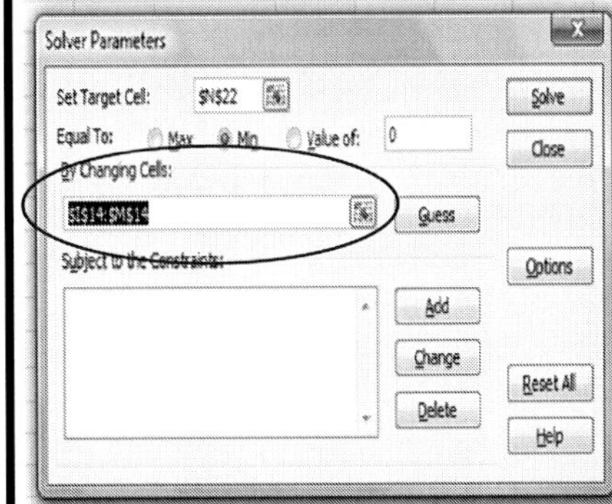
</td>
</tr>
<tr>
<td colspan="3">(Specifies the cells that can be adjusted until the constraints in the problem are satisfied and the cell in the Set Target Cell box reaches its target)</td>
</tr>
<tr>
<td>Subject to the Constraints</td>
<td>$\sum_{j=1}^{n} R_j X_j \geq D$
$\sum_{j=1}^{n} X_j = 1$

$X_j \geq 0$
$j = 1, \ldots, n$</td>
<td>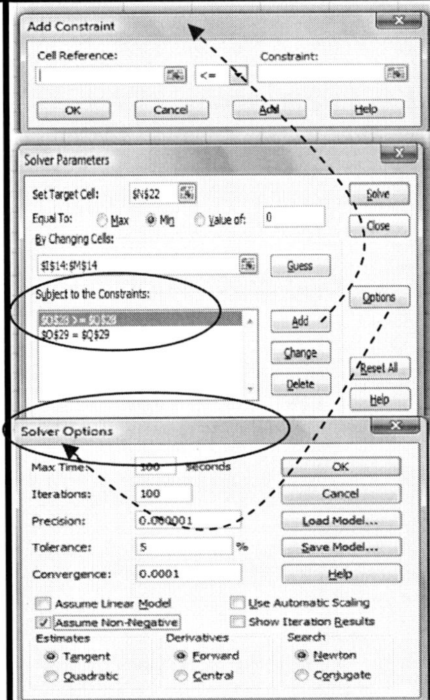
</td>
</tr>
<tr>
<td colspan="3">(In the Solver Options dialogue box, a check box for "Assume Non-Negative" is checked to indicate that the decision variables are not negative)</td>
</tr>
</table>

Step 3: The final step is to click on "solve" for the Excel Solver to find the optimal solution which is the value of the decision variables x_j .

3.3 Goal Programming

3.3.1 The Model

Goal Programming was first used in 1955 by Charnes et al., and developed further by Ignizio (1978), Romero (1991), Schniederjans (1995), Jones and Tamiz (2010) and Tamiz, Azmi and Jones (2013).

Romero (2004) mentions that a key element of a Goal Programming (GP) model is the achievement function, which measures the degree of minimisation of the unwanted deviational variables of the model's goals. Different types of achievement function lead to a different GP.

This book uses the Weighted, Lexicographic and MinMax Goal Programming models for portfolio selection. Other variants for Goal Programming models include Fuzzy GP (Yaghoobi and Tamiz, 2006), Compromise Programming (Yu, 1973) and Stochastic Goal Programming (Abdelaziz, Aouni and El Fayedh, 2007; Aouni and La Torre, 2010).

3.3.1.1 Weighted Goal Programming Model

$$Min \sum_{i=1}^{m} (\alpha_i n_i + \beta_i p_i)$$

Subject to:

$$f_i(\mathbf{x}) + n_i - p_i = b_i \qquad i = 1, .. m$$
$$\mathbf{x} \in C_s$$
$$\mathbf{x} \geq 0, \qquad n_i, p_i \geq 0 \qquad i = 1, .. m$$

Where:
n_i is the ith negative deviational variable.
α_i is the weighting factor for negative deviational variable i.
p_i is the ith positive deviational variable.
β_i is the weighting factor for positive deviational variable i.
$\mathbf{x}$ is the vector of the decision variables.
$f_i(\mathbf{x})$ is the ith objective function.
b_i is the ith target value.

C_s is an optional set of hard constraints.

3.3.1.2 Lexicographic Goal Programming Model

Lex Min **a** =

$$[h_1\left(\sum_{i\in h_1}(\alpha_i n_i + \beta_i p_i)\right), h_2\left(\sum_{i\in h_2}(\alpha_i n_i + \beta_i p_i)\right), \dots, h_q\left(\sum_{i\in h_q}(\alpha_i n_i + \beta_i p_i)\right)]$$

Subject to the same objective functions and constraints of the weighted goal programming model in section 3.3.1.1.

Where:

a is the ordered vector of q priority levels being lexicographically minimised.

3.3.1.3 MinMax Goal Programming Model

Minimise λ

Subject to:

$$\alpha_i n_i + \beta_i p_i \leq \lambda \qquad i = 1, \dots, m$$
$$f_i(\mathbf{x}) + n_i - p_i = b_i \qquad i = 1, \dots, m$$
$$\boldsymbol{x} \in C_s$$
$$\mathbf{x} \geq 0, \qquad n_i, p_i, \lambda \geq 0 \qquad i = 1, \dots, m$$

Where:

λ represents the maximum deviation.

3.3.2 Normalisation Methods

In Goal Programming, when deviational variables are measured in different units and summed directly in the achievement function, incommensurability may occur. The resulting solution may distort the preferences. To overcome incommensurability, normalisation methods are used (Jones and Tamiz, 2010).

Amongst the popular normalisation methods are Percentage Normalisation, Euclidean Normalisation, Summation Normalisation and Zero-One Normalisation. The incommensurability issue occurs in some of the GP models used in this book, specifically in the models used in chapter seven.

In the context of the portfolio selection models in this book, it is found that percentage normalisation is a suitable normalisation method to use.

Percentage normalisation is achieved by dividing deviational variables weights in the achievement function by their respective target values.

For example, the achievement function for the WGP is as follows:

$$Min \sum_{i=1}^{m} (\alpha_i n_i + \beta_i p_i)$$

While the normalised achievement function for the WGP is:

$$Min \sum_{i=1}^{m} (\frac{\alpha_i}{b_i} n_i + \frac{\beta_i}{b_i} p_i)$$

The achievement function for the LGP is:

Lex Min **a** =

$$[h_1(\textstyle\sum_{i \in h_1}(\alpha_i n_i + \beta_i p_i)), h_2(\sum_{i \in h_2}(\alpha_i n_i + \beta_i p_i)), \dots, h_q\left(\sum_{i \in h_q}(\alpha_i n_i + \beta_i p_i)\right)]$$

The normalised achievement function for the LGP is:

Lex Min **a** =

$$[h_1\left(\textstyle\sum_{i \in h_1}(\frac{\alpha_i}{b_i} n_i + \frac{\beta_i}{b_i} p_i)\right), h_2\left(\sum_{i \in h_2}(\frac{\alpha_i}{b_i} n_i + \frac{\beta_i}{b_i} p_i)\right), \dots, h_q\left(\sum_{i \in h_q}(\frac{\alpha_i}{b_i} n_i + \frac{\beta_i}{b_i} p_i)\right)]$$

The relevant part of the MinMax GP model is:

$$\alpha_i n_i + \beta_i p_i \le \lambda \qquad i = 1, \dots, m$$

When normalised this becomes:

$$\frac{\alpha_i}{b_i} n_i + \frac{\beta_i}{b_i} p_i \le \lambda \qquad i = 1, \dots, m$$

3.3.3 Goal Programming Models in the Spreadsheet

3.3.3.1 Weighted Goal Programming Model in the Spreadsheet

Steps for solving the following (normalised) Weighted Goal Programming model using the spreadsheet are set out below:

Step 1: Prepare the Excel sheet for the GP model as shown in the following figure:

Figure 3.2: The Excel sheet for solving the WGP model in the spreadsheet using a general numerical example

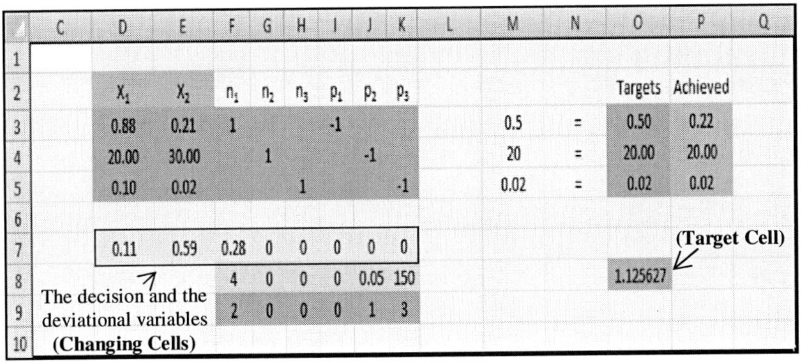

	C	D	E	F	G	H	I	J	K	L	M	N	O	P	Q
1															
2		X_1	X_2	n_1	n_2	n_3	p_1	p_2	p_3				Targets	Achieved	
3		0.88	0.21	1			-1				0.5	=	0.50	0.22	
4		20.00	30.00		1			-1			20	=	20.00	20.00	
5		0.10	0.02			1			-1		0.02	=	0.02	0.02	
6															
7		0.11	0.59	0.28	0	0	0	0	0						
8				4	0	0	0	0.05	150				1.125627		
9				2	0	0	0	1	3						
10															

$$Min\left(\frac{2}{0.50}n_1 + \frac{1}{20}p_2 + \frac{3}{0.02}p_3\right)$$

Subject to:

$$0.88\,X_1 + 0.21\,X_2 + n_1 - p_1 = 0.5$$

$$20\,X_1 + 30\,X_2 + n_2 - p_2 = 20$$

$$0.10\,X_1 + 0.02\,X_2 + n_3 - p_3 = 0.02$$

$$X_1 and\ X_2 \geq 0$$

All the deviational variables ≥ 0

Cells D3 through K5 represent the objectives' coefficients, while Cells M3:M5 represent the left-hand side values of the objectives, namely $f_i(\mathbf{x}) + n_i - p_i$; cells O3:O5 represent the targets for each objective, namely b_i. Cells D7 through K7 are the Changing Cells which represent the values of the decision and the deviational variables.

Normalised weights are computed in this model and are shown in cells F8:K8; cell F8, for example, represents the normalised weight for n_1 and is obtained by dividing its preferred weight, 2 (in cell F9), by its right hand side value, 0.5 (in cell O3).

The Target Cell is indicated in the figure and appears in cell O8 (= SUMPRODUCT (F7:K7, F8:K8)). It represents the weighted sum of the unwanted deviational variables.

Note that cells P3 to P5 represent the achieved values for each objective $f_i(\mathbf{x})$. Each entry for $f_i(\mathbf{x})$ is calculated using the SUMPRODUCT function in Excel. For example, P3= $f_1(\mathbf{x})$ = SUMPRODUCT (D3:E3, D7:E7).

The constraints are taken care of by checking boxes in the Solver Options dialogue box.

Step 2: Set up the Solver dialogue box as illustrated in the following table.

Table 3.2: Weighted Goal Programming model using the spreadsheet

Excel Solver's Parameters	Mathematical representation of the Goal Programming model	Graphical illustration of spreadsheet usage
Set Target Cell	*Min* $\left(\frac{2}{0.50}n_1 + \frac{1}{20}p_2 + \right.$ *30.02p3*	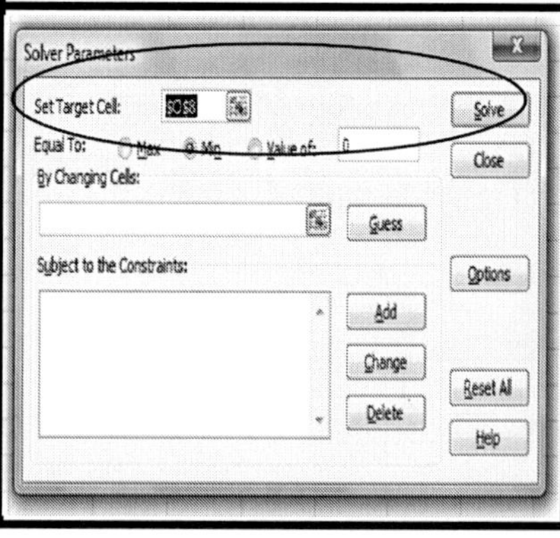

<table>
<tr>
<td>By Changing Cells</td>
<td>$x_1, x_2, n_1, \ldots, p_3$</td>
<td>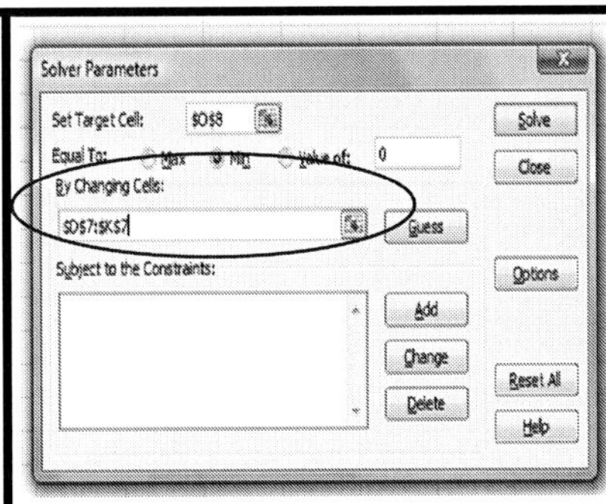
</td>
</tr>
<tr>
<td>Subject to the Constraints</td>
<td>$0.88\,X_1 + 0.21\,X_2 + n_1 - p_1 = 0.5$

$20\,X_1 + 30\,X_2 + n_2 - p_2 = 20$

$0.10\,X_1 + 0.02\,X_2 + n_3 - p_3 = 0.02$

$X_1 and\ X_2 \geq 0$

All the deviational variables ≥ 0</td>
<td>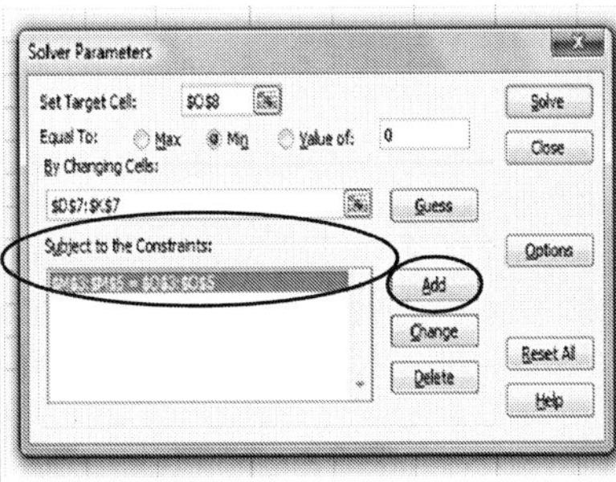

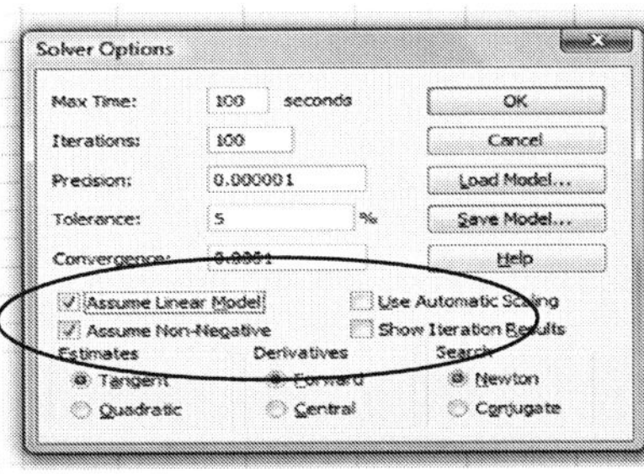
</td>
</tr>
<tr>
<td colspan="3">(In the Solver Options dialogue box, a check box for “Assume Non-Negative” is checked to indicate that the decision variables are not negative. Another check box for “Assume Linear Model” is checked too)</td>
</tr>
</table>

Step 3: Click on “solve” in order for Excel Solver to find the solution.

3.3.3.2 The Lexicographic Goal Programming Model in the Spreadsheet

Given the Lexicographic Goal Programming model:

Lex Min $\boldsymbol{a} = h_1 \left[\frac{2}{0.50} n_1,\ \frac{3}{0.02} p_3\right],\quad h_2 \left[\frac{1}{20} p_2\right]$

Subject to:
$0.88\, X_1 + 0.21\, X_2 + n_1 - p_1 = 0.5$
$20\, X_1 + 30\, X_2 + n_2 - p_2 = 20$
$0.10\, X_1 + 0.02\, X_2 + n_3 - p_3 = 0.02$
$X_1 and\ X_2 \geq 0$
All the deviational variables ≥ 0.

The following are the key steps for solving the model in the spreadsheet.

Step 1: Priority levels should be determined in order to solve a LGP. Building on the same model of WGP (illustrated in figure 3.2), two priority levels are used, and hence the LGP is solved in two steps. The first priority level is to minimise p_3 and n_1 (for example, minimising the positive deviation of risk and minimising the negative deviation of return). The second priority level is to minimise p_2 (for example, minimising the positive deviation of the volatility variable).

Step 2: Insert the weights for the unwanted deviational variables for solving the first priority level as illustrated in the following figure.

Figure 3.3: The Excel sheet prepared for solving the LGP model

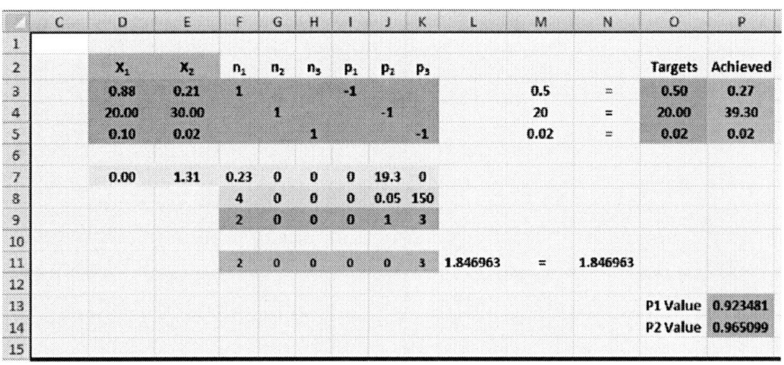

	C	D	E	F	G	H	I	J	K	L	M	N	O	P
1														
2		X_1	X_2	n_1	n_2	n_3	p_1	p_2	p_3				Targets	Achieved
3		0.88	0.21	1			-1				0.5	=	0.50	0.27
4		20.00	30.00		1			-1			20	=	20.00	39.30
5		0.10	0.02			1			-1		0.02	=	0.02	0.02
6														
7		0.00	1.31	0.23	0	0	0	19.3	0					
8				4	0	0	0	0.05	150					
9				2	0	0	0	1	3					
10														
11				2	0	0	0	0	3	1.846963	=	1.846963		
12														
13													P1 Value	0.923481
14													P2 Value	0.965099
15														

Figure 3.3 shows the weights for the unwanted deviational variables used for priority level 1, which are in cells F11:K11. This priority level

(P1) is solved using the same steps as in WGP (in section 3.3.3.1) except for:

- The weights for n_1 and p_3 are inserted only in this priority level.
- The Target Cell equals the SUMPRODUCT function in Excel for the cells relevant only to the priority level 1's variables. For example, cell P13 is made up of: SUMPRODUCT(F7,F8)+SUMPRODUCT(H7:I7,H8:I8)+ SUMPRODUCT(K7,K8).

Step 3: Solve the first priority level of LGP (following the same procedures as in table 3.2 and save the solution as the P1 value (cell P13 in figure 3.3).

Step 4: Introduce the Target Cell P14 which equals the SUMPRODUCT of the deviational variables of the second priority level only, which are n_2 and p_2 (P14= SUMPRODUCT (G7,G8) + SUMPRODUCT (J7,J8).

Step 5: Solve the second priority level of LGP, adding the level 1 solution obtained from previous steps as a constraint.

The following table summarises the solution steps for the priority level two.

Table 3.3: Lexicographic Goal Programming model using the spreadsheet

Excel Solver's Parameters	Mathematical representation of the Goal Programming model	Graphical illustration of spreadsheet usage
Set Target Cell (Cell P14 in figure 3.3)	Lex Min a= $[h_1(n,p), h_2(n,p)]$ ($h_2(n,p)$ represent P2 which is the priority level minimised in this step of the current example)	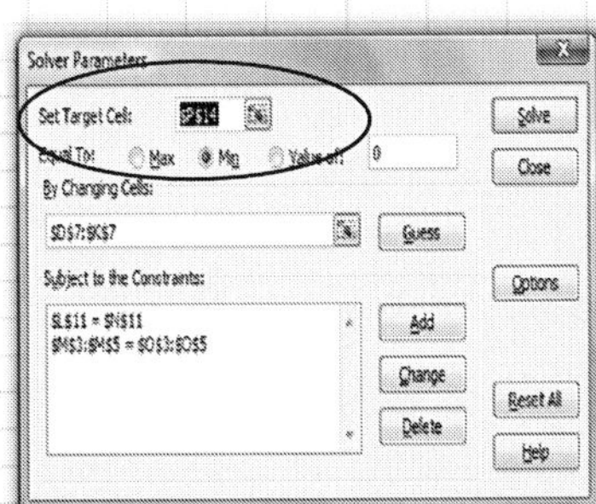

<table>
<tr>
<td>By Changing Cells

(Cells D7:K7 in figure 3.3)</td>
<td>$X_i, n_{i'}$ and $p_{i'}$</td>
<td>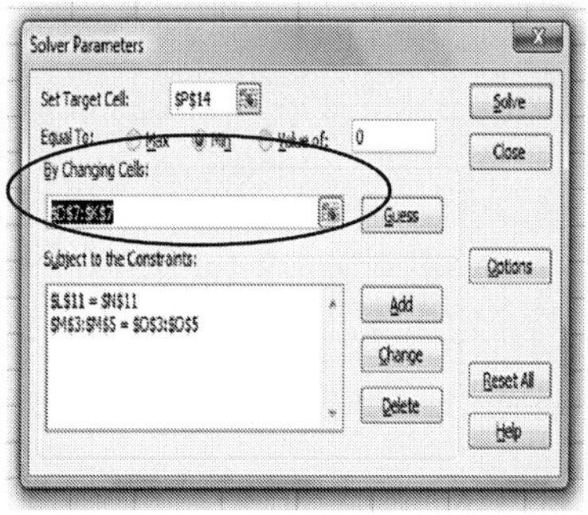
</td>
</tr>
<tr>
<td>Subject to the Constraints</td>
<td>$f_i(\mathbf{x}) + n_i - p_i = b_i$

$\boldsymbol{x} \geq 0$

$n_i, p_i \geq 0 \quad i = 1, \ldots m$</td>
<td>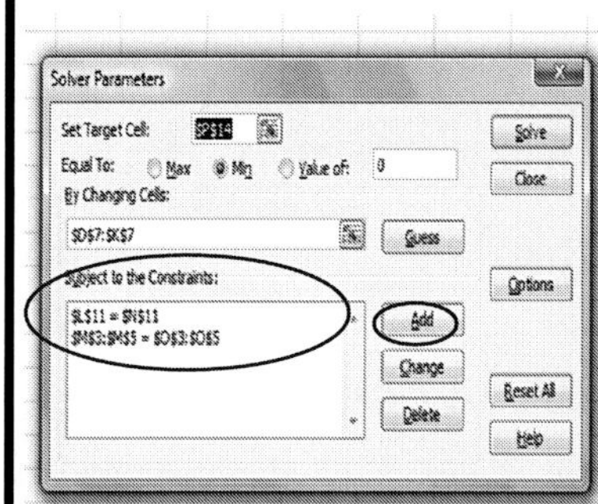

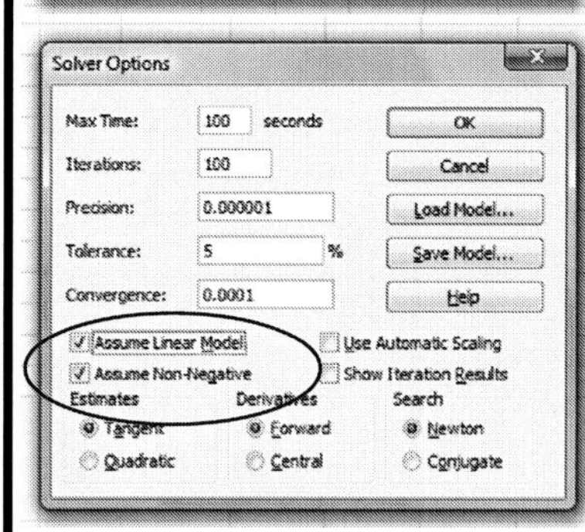
</td>
</tr>
<tr>
<td colspan="3">The constraint that cell L11=N11 (as shown in figure 3.3) is the constraint added in the P2 model for solving the LGP of two priority levels. Constraint M3:M5=O3:O5 (as shown in figure 3.3) is already in the model since solving the P1 step.</td>
</tr>
</table>

3.3.3.3 The MinMax Goal Programming Model in the Spreadsheet

The following are the key steps for solving the MinMax Goal Programming model in the spreadsheet (given the following MinMax GP model):

Step 1: Based on the previous WGP model, the first step in solving a MinMax GP model in Excel is to add n_1, n_2, n_3 and p_1, p_2, p_3 to λ as illustrated in the following figure (as per the mathematical model below):

Minimise λ

Subject to:

$$\frac{2}{0.50}n_1 - \lambda \leq 0$$

$$\frac{1}{20}p_2 - \lambda \leq 0$$

$$\frac{3}{0.02}p_3 - \lambda \leq 0$$

$$0.88\,X_1 + 0.21\,X_2 + n_1 - p_1 = 0.5$$

$$20\,X_1 + 30\,X_2 + n_2 - p_2 = 20$$

$$0.10\,X_1 + 0.02\,X_2 + n_3 - p_3 = 0.02$$

$$X_1 and\ X_2 \geq 0$$

All the deviational variables ≥ 0

Figure 3.4: The Excel sheet prepared for solving the MinMax GP model

	C	D	E	F	G	H	I	J	K	L	M	N	O	P	Q	R
1										λ						
2		X_1	X_2	n_1	n_2	n_3	p_1	p_2	p_3	Lambda				Targets	Achieved	
3		0.88	0.21	1			-1					0.5	=	0.50	0.30	
4		20.00	30.00		1			-1				20	=	20.00	35.73	
5		0.10	0.02			1			-1			0.02	=	0.02	0.03	
6				1			1			-1		0	<=	0	0.00	
7					1			1		-1		0	<=	0	0.00	
8						1			1	-1		0	<=	0	0.00	
9																
10		0.08	1.14	0.2	0	0	0	15.7	0	0.7865						
11				4	0	0	0	0.05	150	1				0.78655		
12				2	0	0	0	1	3							
13																

Figure 3.4 shows the added rows for MinMax GP's n_s (cells F6:H8) and p_s (cells I6:K8) with their corresponding λ_s (L6:L8).

Step 2: Redefine the Target Cell to be equal to the changing cell of (λ) Lambda (P11= L10). Also, redefine the Changing Cells to include the data of Lambda.

Step 3: Solve the model using Excel Solver as illustrated in the following table.

Table 3.4: MinMax Goal Programming model using the spreadsheet

Excel Solver's Parameters	Mathematical representation of the Goal Programming model	Graphical illustration of spreadsheet usage
Set Target Cell (Cell P14 in figure 3.3)	Minimise λ	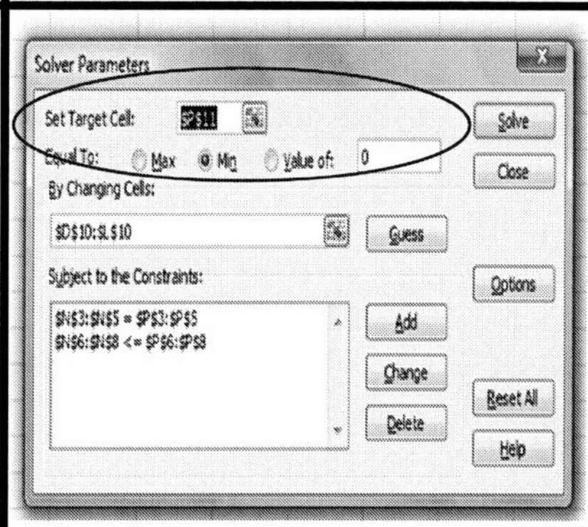
By Changing Cells (Cells D7:K7 in figure 3.3)	X_i, n_i, p_i *and* λ	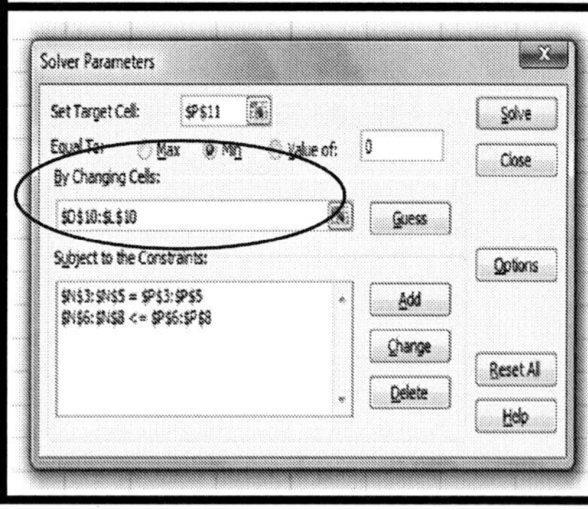

<table>
<tr>
<td>Subject to the Constraints</td>
<td>

$\alpha_i n_i + \beta_i p_i \leq \lambda$

$f_i(\mathbf{x}) + n_i - p_i = b_i$

$\boldsymbol{x} \geq 0$

$n_i, p_i \geq 0 \quad i = 1,..m$

</td>
<td>

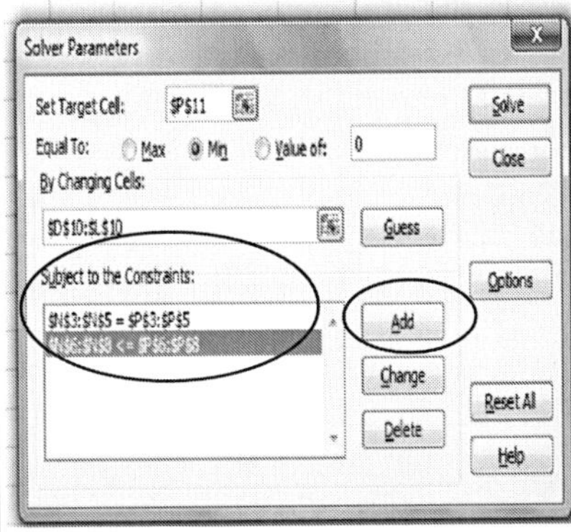

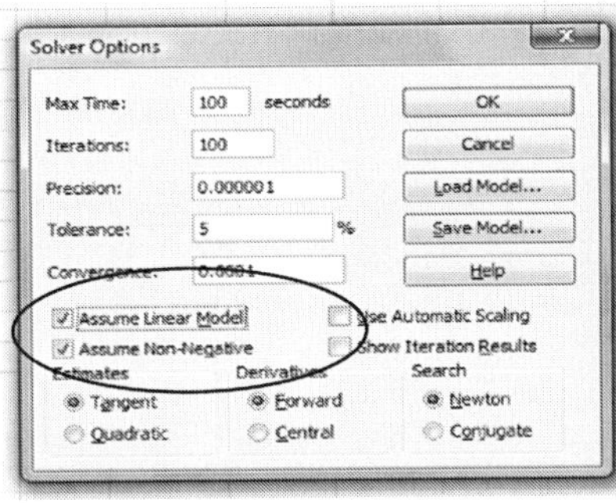

</td>
</tr>
</table>

3.4 Konno's Methodology

3.4.1 The Model

Konno and Yamazaki (1991) propose an alternative to Markowitz's Mean-Variance (M-V) model; this is the Mean-Absolute Deviation (MAD) model, which can be formulated and solved as a Weighted Goal Programming problem. The M-V model assumes normality of stock returns, while the MAD model does not make this assumption. The MAD model also minimises a measure of risk, where the measure in this case is the mean absolute deviation. Konno and Yamazaki (1991) show that L_1 risk model can be used as an alternative to Markowitz's L_2 risk model (1952).

In particular, Konno and Yamazaki (1991) show that the Mean-Absolute Deviation is equivalent to the Mean-Variance and then they convert the Absolute Deviation to a GP model. Building on Konno's methodology, this book applies his model using a relevant benchmark to measure the risk instead of the mean return. The model used is represented mathematically as follows:

$$Min \sum_{t=1}^{k} (n_t + p_t)$$

Subject to:

$$\sum_{j=1}^{m} (R_{jt} - I_t)X_j + n_t - p_t = 0 \qquad t = 1, \dots, k$$

$$\sum_{j=1}^{m} X_j = 1$$

$$X_j \geq 0 \qquad j = 1, \dots, m \qquad n_t, p_t \geq 0 \qquad t = 1, \dots, k$$

Where:
R_{jt}= Return of the jth asset during period *t*.
I_t = Return of the relevant index during period *t*.
X_j= The proportion of the jth asset selected.
n_t= The negative deviational variable for period *t*.
p_t = The positive deviational variable for period *t*.

This model is designed so that the sum of deviations from the benchmark (index) is minimised. A benchmark is a standard against which the performance of a security, mutual fund or investment manager can be measured. Generally, a broad market index is used for this purpose.

3.4.2 The Model in the Spreadsheet

Note that the WGP used for solving Konno's model does not require preferred weights for the unwanted deviational variables. Also, as all the objectives are measured with the same unit of measurement it does not require any type of normalisation techniques as described in Tamiz and Jones (1997). Therefore, a specialised Excel sheet is used for solving Konno's model as follows.

Figure 3.5: The Excel sheet used in solving Konno's model

J30 =SUM(I7:J27)

	C	D	E	F	G	H	I	J	K	L	M	N
3									The decision variables			
4						1.00	=	1	(Changing Cells)			
5	X_1	X_2	X_3	X_4	X_5							
6	0.15	0.15	0.15	0.40	0.15							
7	-0.00312	0.00082	-0.01326	-0.01920	-0.00473	-0.01073	0.01	0.00	0.00	=	0	
8	0.04239	0.02601	0.02484	0.01946	0.02528	0.02556	0.00	0.03	0.00	=	0	
9	0.05728	-0.00414	0.01206	0.00068	-0.00553	0.00922	0.00	0.01	0.00	=	0	
10	0.01364	-0.00843	-0.00348	-0.00750	-0.00331	-0.00324	0.00	0.00	0.00	=	0	
11	0.07403	0.00729	0.02336	0.00570	0.01388	0.02006	0.00	0.02	0.00	=	0	
12	-0.04532	0.01084	-0.01637	0.01394	0.01025	-0.00051	0.00	0.00	0.00	=	0	
13	0.02501	-0.00826	-0.01932	-0.01892	-0.02555	-0.01179	0.01	0.00	0.00	=	0	
14	0.03336	0.02020	-0.00134	0.00756	0.00760	0.01200	0.00	0.01	0.00	=	0	
15	-0.02023	0.03185	0.02559	0.02577	0.02389	0.01947	0.00	0.02	0.00	=	0	
16	-0.00676	-0.02690	-0.01429	-0.02948	-0.02259	-0.02237	0.02	0.00	0.00	=	0	
17	0.00962	0.02868	0.01938	0.01525	0.01221	0.01658	0.00	0.02	0.00	=	0	
18	-0.00625	-0.02344	-0.01913	-0.01544	-0.00698	-0.01455	0.01	0.00	0.00	=	0	
19	0.01239	0.02665	0.01205	0.01546	0.01532	0.01614	0.00	0.02	0.00	=	0	
20	-0.00549	-0.00506	-0.01405	-0.00012	-0.01443	-0.00590	0.01	0.00	0.00	=	0	
21	-0.00106	0.00025	0.01170	-0.00382	0.00127	0.00030	0.00	0.00	0.00	=	0	
22	0.02163	0.00502	-0.00714	0.00613	0.00510	0.00614	0.00	0.01	0.00	=	0	
23	0.00860	-0.00286	0.00586	0.00458	-0.00103	0.00342	0.00	0.00	0.00	=	0	
24	0.02240	-0.00136	-0.00561	0.00188	-0.00126	0.00288	0.00	0.00	0.00	=	0	
25	-0.01697	0.00596	0.00301	0.00086	-0.00110	-0.00102	0.00	0.00	0.00	=	0	
26	0.00834	-0.00767	-0.00033	-0.00273	-0.01052	-0.00262	0.00	0.00	0.00	=	0	
27	0.03736	-0.00052	0.00235	0.00418	0.00763	0.00869	0.00	0.01	0.00	=	0	
28								The Objective Function value				
29									(Target Cell)			
30								0.21				

In figure 3.5, cells C7 through G27 represent the data, while cells H7 to H27 represent the achievement value for objectives, $f_i(x)$. Each entry for $f_i(x)$ is calculated using the SUMPRODUCT function in Excel. For example, H7= $f_1(x)$ = SUMPRODUCT (C6:G6, C7:G7).

Cells I7 through J27 are the representation of the negative and positive deviational variables (n_i and p_i). Cells K7:K27 represent the left-hand side values of the objectives $(R_{jt} - I_t)X_j + n_t - p_t = 0$, while cells M7:M27 represent the targets for each objective (= 0).

The Excel Solver is the key tool used to find a solution to Konno's model as shown in the following table:

Table 3.5: Konno's model using the spreadsheet

<table>
<tr><th>Excel Solver's Parameters</th><th>Mathematical representation of Konno's model</th><th>Graphical illustration of spreadsheet usage</th></tr>
<tr><td>Set Target Cell</td><td>$Min \sum_{t=1}^{k} (n_t + p_t)$</td><td>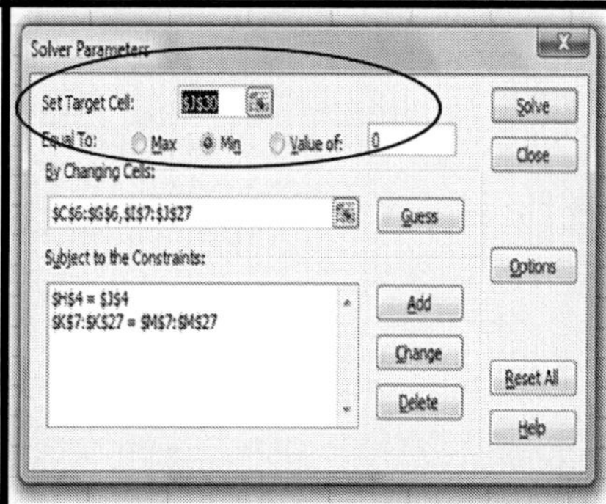
</td></tr>
<tr><td>By Changing Cells</td><td>n_t, p_t and X_j</td><td>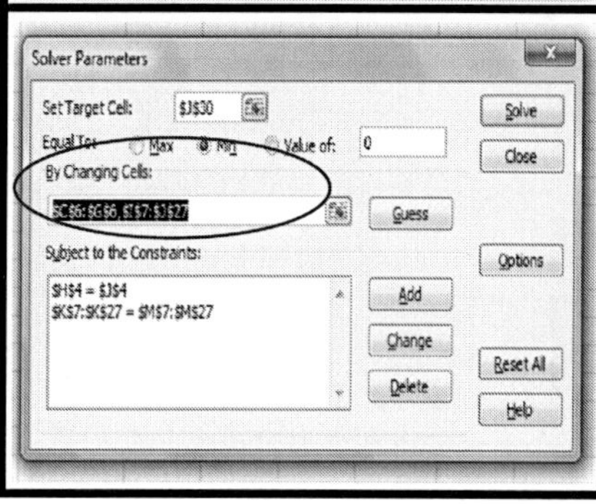
</td></tr>
</table>

Subject to the Constraints	$\sum_{j=1}^{m}(R_{jt} - I_t)X_j + n_t - p_t = 0$ $\sum_{j=1}^{m} X_j = 1$ $X_j \geq 0$ $j = 1, \dots, m$ $n_t, p_t \geq 0$ $t = 1, \dots, k$	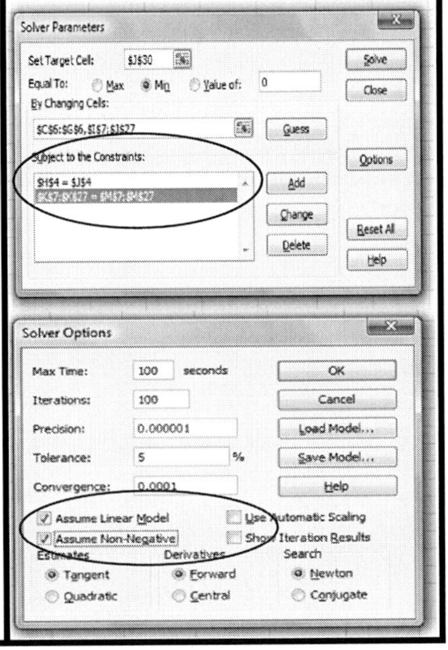

3.5 Sharpe Methodology

3.5.1 The Model

Sharpe (1966), together with Treynor (1965) and Jensen (1968), developed the standard indices to measure risk-adjusted returns for portfolios.

Jensen index, or Jensen's Alpha, which measures the deviation of a portfolio from the securities market line, has been the focus of controversy over whether it provides investors with superior information to help in portfolio selection decisions. One criticism of the Jensen measure is that it is based on an upwardly biased estimate of systematic risk for a market-timing investment strategy (Grinblatt and Titman, 1989).

This chapter employs the main methods of measuring return per unit of risk for assets (and ranking them) as follows:

- The reward to variability ratio (Sharpe Ratio) developed by William Sharpe (1966).
- The reward to volatility ratio (Treynor ratio) developed by Jack Treynor (1965).

The ranking according to both measures will be identical, when the assets under consideration are perfectly diversified or at least highly diversified. However, the rankings of the two measures will diverge when the assets being appraised are less highly diversified.

The Sharpe Ratio (the higher the ratio, the better the performance of the corresponding asset) is the ratio of the realised asset return in excess of the risk-free rate to the variability of return as measured by the standard deviation.

Various refinements to the Sharpe ratio have been suggested and recently discussed in the literature (for instance, Scholz, 2007). In the context of portfolio selection, Balbas, Balbas and Mayoral (2009) show that a feasible portfolio can be outperformed by adequately combining the riskless asset and the strategy maximising the generalised Sharpe ratio. This is a special strategy that composes the efficient portfolios in a new risk/return framework.

However, this book utilises the Sharpe ratio, as described in Sharpe (1966), to rank and select assets in a portfolio; this is for the following main reasons:

- The viability of comparison with the Treynor ratio, since the two performance ratios differ only in as much as one measures total risk by the standard deviation (Sharpe) while the other measures market risk by the portfolio beta. Treynor (1965) assumes that a portfolio manager should be able to diversify and eliminate all the unsystematic risk.
- The ability to introduce a standardised approach to decide on portfolio constituents' proportions, given the selection of the constituents by Sharpe and Treynor. This standardised approach is described later in this chapter as "Weighting Algorithms," in section 3.7.

Based on an assets ranking according to the Sharpe or Treynor ratios, a portfolio of best assets could be built.

The Sharpe basic ratio is computed as follows:

$$\mathrm{S}_j = \frac{\mathrm{R}_j - \mathrm{R}_f}{\mathrm{SD}_j} \qquad j = 1, \dots, n$$

Where:

S_j= Sharpe Ratio for the jth asset, $j = 1, \dots, n$.
R_j= Return of the jth asset.

R_f = The risk-free rate.
SD_j= Standard deviation of the jth asset.

3.5.2 The Model in the Spreadsheet

The following are the key steps for portfolio selection using the Sharpe method in a spreadsheet:

Step 1: Prepare the Excel sheet of the required data for computing the Sharpe ratio of the available assets in order to rank them as shown in the following figure.

Figure 3.6: The data prepared for computing the Sharpe ratio using a simple numerical example

	D	E	F	G	H	I	J	K	L	M	N
115					Assets Data						Risk Free Rate
116	-0.02958	-0.02751	-0.02752	-0.01970	-0.04536	-0.02769	-0.04690	-0.02951	-0.02973	-0.04828	0.05500
117	0.02816	0.02339	0.03360	0.02998	0.03741	0.03889	0.04691	0.03392	0.02225	0.04587	0.05500
118	-0.01047	-0.01595	-0.01332	-0.01561	-0.02038	-0.01913	-0.00870	-0.01980	-0.01659	-0.02525	0.05500
119	-0.01824	-0.00054	-0.00499	-0.00718	-0.01372	-0.00776	-0.00662	-0.01904	0.00564	-0.01772	0.05500
120	0.02090	0.00649	0.02278	0.01133	0.02794	0.02688	0.02433	0.03588	0.00799	0.04025	0.05750
121	0.00926	0.00913	0.01001	0.00373	0.00789	0.00900	0.00667	0.00568	0.00110	0.00534	0.05750
122	-0.00982	-0.00745	-0.01021	-0.00468	-0.00515	-0.00965	-0.01018	-0.00903	-0.01272	-0.00995	0.05750
123	-0.04894	-0.03646	-0.06172	-0.05361	-0.06725	-0.06051	-0.07642	-0.06268	-0.05167	-0.07909	0.05750
124	0.01179	0.01169	0.00694	0.00767	0.01447	0.00339	0.02670	0.00669	0.00560	0.01674	0.05750
125											
126											
127	MF_1	MF_2	MF_3	MF_4	MF_5	MF_6	MF_7	MF_8	MF_9	MF_{10}	$j=10$
128											
129	7	10	6	8	3	5	2	4	9	1	
130											
131	-2.460	-3.099	-2.162	-2.625	-1.872	-2.076	-1.613	-2.015	-2.826	-1.592	
132											
133	-0.5%	-0.4%	-0.5%	-0.5%	-0.7%	-0.5%	-0.5%	-0.6%	-0.8%	-0.8%	
134	0.06	0.06	0.06	0.06	0.06	0.06	0.06	0.06	0.06	0.06	
135	0.03	0.02	0.03	0.02	0.03	0.03	0.04	0.03	0.02	0.04	

Figure 3.6 shows the data available for the assets to be included in the portfolio (cells D116:N124). Cells D133 to M133 represent the average return for each asset (R_j in section 3.5.1), which is calculated for each asset using the AVERAGE function in Excel from the data in cells D116 through M124. Cells D134:M134 represent R_f (calculated using the AVERAGE function for the cells N116:N124), while cells D135:M135 represent the SD_j in section 3.5.1 (which is calculated using the STDEVA function). The Sharpe ratio is calculated for the 10 assets using the model in section 3.5.1 (cells D131:M131).

Step 2: The assets are ranked according to their Sharpe ratio in cells D129 through M129 (figure 3.6) using the RANK function in Excel. Then the top-ranked ones are selected based on the required number of assets in a portfolio.

Step 3: Use one of the weighting algorithms that are detailed in section 3.7 in order to obtain the proportions for the assets selected in step 2.

3.6 Treynor Methodology

3.6.1 The Model

The Treynor ratio, or the reward to volatility ratio, as developed by Jack Treynor (1965), is the ratio between the realised portfolio return in excess of the risk-free rate, and the volatility of return as measured by the portfolio beta.

Although Jensen measures the risk-adjusted returns based on systematic risk, as is the case with the Treynor ratio (both use the securities market line), this book deploys the Treynor approach in portfolio selection for the following main reasons:

- The aim of using either the Treynor or Jensen approaches is to incorporate the systematic risk in portfolio choice and then to compare this with other methods. Treynor is more suitable for comparison with the Sharpe ratio, as detailed in section 3.5.1.
- Although the Jensen approach uses the same measure of risk as in Treynor, the Jensen index (alpha) uses the Capital Asset Pricing Model as a basis to determine whether a portfolio outperforms the market index as follows:

$$J_j^{\alpha} = \mathrm{R}_j - (\mathrm{R}_f + Beta_j\,(\mathrm{RM} - \mathrm{R}_f))$$

Where:

J_j^{α} = Jensen's Alpha for the jth asset, $j = 1, \ldots, n$.

$Beta_j$ = Beta Coefficient of the jth asset.

RM = The market return.

The data for a relevant benchmark is required and used twice in the above equation (once as part of the beta measurement and again as an estimate for market return). This is compared to the use of relevant benchmark data only once in the Treynor ratio.

- Furthermore, the ultimate aim of using any of the risk-adjusted measures is the meaningful comparison with other relevant methods based on the book's focus.

The Treynor Ratio is computed as follows:

$$T_j = \frac{R_j - R_f}{Beta_j} \qquad j = 1, \dots, n$$

Where:
T_j = Treynor Ratio for the jth asset, $j = 1, \dots, n$.
$Beta_j$ = Beta Coefficient of the jth asset.
The Beta Coefficient, as a measure of systematic risk, is computed as follows (Miller, 2002):

$$Beta_j = \frac{\mathrm{Cov}\left(R_j, RM\right)}{\sigma_m^2}$$

$$Beta_j = \frac{\sum_{t=1}^{n}(R_{jt} - \bar{R}_{jt})(RM_t - \overline{RM}_t)}{\sum_{t=1}^{n}(RM_t - \overline{RM}_t)^2}$$

Where:
$Beta_j$ = The Beta Coefficient of the jth asset.
$\mathrm{Cov}\left(R_j, RM\right)$ = Covariance between the return of the jth asset and the return of the market portfolio RM.
σ_m^2 = Variance in the return of market's portfolio.
R_{jt} = The return of the jth asset during the period t.
$\bar{R}_{jt}$ = The average return of the jth asset during the period t.
RM_t = The market return during the period t.
$\overline{RM}_t$ = The average return of the market portfolio during the period t.

3.6.2 The Model in the Spreadsheet

The following are the key steps for portfolio selection using the Treynor method in a spreadsheet:

Step 1: Prepare the Excel sheet of the required data for computing the Treynor's ratio of the available assets in order to rank them as shown in the following figure.

Figure 3.7: The data prepared for computing the Treynor ratio using a simple numerical example

	C	D	E	F	G	H	I	J	K	L	M	N
115	Benchmark					Assets Data						Risk Free Rate
116	-0.03	-0.03	-0.03	-0.03	-0.02	-0.05	-0.03	-0.05	-0.03	-0.03	-0.05	0.06
117	0.03	0.03	0.02	0.03	0.03	0.04	0.04	0.05	0.03	0.02	0.05	0.06
118	-0.02	-0.01	-0.02	-0.01	-0.02	-0.02	-0.02	-0.01	-0.02	-0.02	-0.03	0.06
119	0.01	-0.02	0.00	0.00	-0.01	-0.01	-0.01	-0.01	-0.02	0.01	-0.02	0.06
120	0.01	0.02	0.01	0.02	0.01	0.03	0.03	0.02	0.04	0.01	0.04	0.06
121	0.00	0.01	0.01	0.01	0.00	0.01	0.01	0.01	0.01	0.00	0.01	0.06
122	-0.02	-0.01	-0.01	-0.01	0.00	-0.01	-0.01	-0.01	-0.01	-0.01	-0.01	0.06
123	-0.06	-0.05	-0.04	-0.06	-0.05	-0.07	-0.06	-0.08	-0.06	-0.05	-0.08	0.06
124	0.00	0.01	0.01	0.01	0.01	0.01	0.00	0.03	0.01	0.01	0.02	0.06
125	-0.01	-0.01	0.00	0.00	-0.01	-0.01	-0.01	0.00	-0.01	-0.01	-0.01	0.06
126												
127		MF_1	MF_2	MF_3	MF_4	MF_5	MF_6	MF_7	MF_8	MF_9	MF_{10}	j=10
128												
129		8	10	6	7	3	4	2	5	9	1	
130												
131		-0.074	-0.088	-0.060	-0.074	-0.054	-0.058	-0.047	-0.059	-0.077	-0.046	
132												
133		-0.5%	-0.4%	-0.5%	-0.5%	-0.7%	-0.5%	-0.5%	-0.6%	-0.8%	-0.8%	
134		0.06	0.06	0.06	0.06	0.06	0.06	0.06	0.06	0.06	0.06	
135		0.84	0.69	1.02	0.84	1.17	1.07	1.31	1.06	0.83	1.40	

Figure 3.7 shows the data available for the assets to be included in the portfolio (cells C116:N125 including cells C125 through N125 which are the average values for each column). Cells D133 to M133 represent the average return for each asset (R_j in section 3.6.1), which is calculated for each asset using the AVERAGE function in Excel from the data in cells D116 through M124. Cells D134:M134 represent R_f, while cells D135:M135 represent $Beta_j$ in section 3.6.1.

For example:
D135=$Beta_1$=(SUMPRODUCT ((D116:D124-D$125), ($C$116:$C$124-$C$125))/ SUMPRODUCT(($C$116:$C$124-$C$125), ($C$116:$C$124-$C$125))), which is the representation of the beta equation in section 3.6.1. The Treynor ratio is calculated for the 10 assets using the model in section 3.6.1 (cells D131:M131).

Step 2: The assets are ranked according to their Treynor ratio in cells D129 through M129 (figure 3.7) using the RANK function in Excel. Then the top-ranked ones are selected based on the required number of assets in a portfolio.

Step 3: Use one of the weighting algorithms that are detailed in section 3.7 in order to obtain the weights for the assets selected in step 2.

3.7 Weighting Algorithms

Some portfolio selection methods, such as Sharpe and Treynor, identify the desired assets for the portfolio, but not their proportions. The weighting algorithms are therefore developed for finding the proportions of such portfolio constituents. In these algorithms V_i represents the assigned value to the ith asset and X_i represents its proportion.

3.7.1 Algorithm (1)

The weighting algorithm for values that are all positive is as follows:

$$V_i > 0 \qquad i = 1, \dots, n$$

$$X_i = \left[\frac{V_i}{\sum_{i=1}^{n} V_i}\right] \times 100\% \qquad i = 1, \dots, n$$

3.7.2 Algorithm (2)

The weighting algorithm for values that are all negative is as follows:

$$V_i < 0 \qquad i = 1, \dots, n$$

$$V_i' = \frac{1}{|V_i|}$$

$$X_i = \left[\frac{V_i'}{\sum_{i=1}^{n} V_i'}\right] \times 100\% \qquad i = 1, \dots, n$$

This algorithm ensures that the order of importance is preserved (i.e., the larger the value, the higher the weight).

3.7.3 Algorithm (3)

If some of the values are positive while the rest are negative, the proportions can be obtained using either of the following algorithms:

3.7.3.1 Algorithm (3.1)

$V_i > 0 \quad i = 1, \ldots, k \qquad V_i < 0 \quad i = k+1, \ldots, n$

$V_i' = V_i \qquad i = 1, \ldots, k$

$V_i' = \frac{1}{|V_i|} \qquad i = k+1, \ldots, n$

$$X_i = \left[\frac{V_i'}{\sum_{i=1}^{n} V_i'}\right] \times 100\% \qquad i = 1, \ldots, n$$

3.7.3.2 Algorithm (3.2)

$V_i > 0 \quad i = 1, \ldots, k \qquad V_i < 0 \quad i = k+1, \ldots, n$

$$X_i = \left[\frac{V_i + C}{nC + \sum_{i=1}^{n} V_i}\right] \times 100\% \qquad i = 1, \ldots, n$$

Where:
C is a large enough scaling factor that is added to all the values to ensure that they are all positive.

The suggested algorithms are all useful in finding the relevant proportions from any assigned values to portfolio constituents. Such values can be assigned using any financial criteria of relevance to decision makers' aims in selecting their portfolios.

All algorithms are designed to ensure that each constituent's value is assigned a corresponding proportion that reflects its importance or ranking within a portfolio. This is the main advantage of using such weighting algorithms.

In particular, algorithm (1) is beneficial in assigning appropriate proportions by which it can preserve the relative importance of each constituent if their values are positive. If the constituents' values are negative, however, algorithm (1) is no longer useful (especially in preserving the relative importance) and that is why algorithm (2) is introduced. The main advantage of algorithm (2) is that it keeps the relevant constituent rank within a portfolio by assigning the corresponding proportion, even though the constituent values are all negative. Algorithms (3.1) and (3.2) are both practical in deciding on the proportions from constituent values that include both positive and negative values. Algorithm (3.2) is easier and quicker for computations compared to algorithm (3.1). However, algorithm (3.1) is more accurate, since algorithm (3.2) requires adding a large enough scaling factor.

Which of the three algorithms we choose to use depends on the particular values assigned to the portfolio constituents (whether positive, negative or both) in order to ensure efficiency in finding the suitable proportions.

CHAPTER FOUR

PORTFOLIO SELECTION APPLICATIONS FOR MUTUAL FUNDS

4.1 Introduction

Mutual funds today are the most popular way to invest in stock markets. Over the last two decades the mutual fund industry has experienced extraordinary growth in many parts of the world. For example, the national association of U.S. investment companies emphasises that mutual funds are the most commonly held type of funds, even after the onset of the current crisis. The U.S. mutual fund market, with about $10 trillion in assets under management for 93 million U.S. investors as of year-end 2008 (compared to $13 trillion at year-end 2007), remained the largest in the world, although their net assets fell reflecting the sharp drop in equity prices experienced worldwide in 2008. The U.S. mutual funds account for 51% of the $19 trillion in mutual fund assets worldwide, while European mutual funds account for 33% (Bliss, Potter and Schwarz, 2008; ICI, 2009).

As of 2005 the market value of the stocks held in mutual fund portfolios accounted for nearly 22% of total U.S. stock market capitalisation, versus 5% at the close of 1985. In response to this trend, as well as to other incentives, financial intermediaries acting as fund managers are increasingly offering mutual funds based on a portfolio of other mutual funds, which is called "funds of funds." The growth in the variety of mutual funds available to investors plays an important role in explaining the existence and growth of funds of funds (Gregoriou, 2007).

Evaluating the performance of mutual funds is increasingly important in light of the continued growth in their number and the intense competition among them for new capital, particularly after the onset of the current crisis (Dor et al., 2008).

Woerheide (1982) suggests some criteria that might be used by investors to select a mutual fund once they have decided on an investment objective. These include investor examination of prior rates of return. However, prior rate of return (using net asset value) is only one ingredient in mutual fund performance.

It is assumed that the basic objective of a mutual fund is to provide a diversified portfolio so as to reduce the risk in investments at a lower cost. Hence, one of the major methods of assessing mutual fund performance is to relate the absolute level of realised return to the level of risk incurred. According to this method, low-return funds would rank better than high-return funds if the risk incurred in earning the return was sufficiently low for the low-return funds as compared to the high-return funds. Treynor (1965), Sharpe (1966) and Jensen (1968) develop the standard indices to measure risk-adjusted returns for portfolios.

The original portfolio selection problem involving risk and return analysis can be modelled as a Goal Programming (GP) model with two objectives. This makes GP helpful in achieving the competing goals in constructing funds with multiple objectives. More applications of GP to portfolio selection are provided by Lee and Lerro (1973), Kumar et al. (1978), Levary and Avery (1984), Tamiz et al. (1996), Inuiguchi and Ramik (2000), Pendaraki et al. (2005), Gladish et al. (2007), and Wu et al. (2007).

4.2 Data and Time Periods

This chapter provides a methodology to analyse a portfolio of mutual funds in two consecutive time periods; namely, the "constructing" period and the "testing" period. Two different markets are examined in two different time periods representing both stable and volatile times in relative terms.

In the United Kingdom, as in most countries (developed and emerging), the deterioration in financial markets began with the onset of the current financial and economic crisis in late 2007. The crisis phase of mid-September to end-October 2008 saw the lion's share of the collapse with most market indices as well as mutual fund rate of returns falling 30% to 40% (Bartram and Bodnar, 2009).

Therefore, for the experiment in the context of the UK's mutual funds, 88 weeks' data, from June 2007 to January 2009, are used to rank, select and construct portfolios. Subsequently, the period from February 2009 to June 2009 (20 weeks) is used to test and compare constructed portfolios (using the FTSE 100 index as the benchmark).

The overall time period selected for the experiment with the UK's mutual funds (from June 2007 to June 2009) includes different phases within the financial and economic crisis. In particular, BIS (2009) mentions that the crisis has developed in five distinct stages, starting with the subprime mortgage-related turmoil between June 2007 and mid-March

2008, in which the primary focus was on funding liquidity and bank losses. In the second stage, from March to mid-September 2008, funding problems morphed into concerns about solvency, giving rise to the risk of outright bank failures. One such failure, the demise of Lehman Brothers on 15 September 2008, triggered the third and most intense stage of the crisis (Teresiene and Paskevicius, 2009), which is a global loss of confidence. Stage four, from late October 2008 to mid-March 2009, witnessed gloomy global growth outlooks amid uncertainties over the effects of ongoing government intervention in markets and the economy. Stage five, beginning in mid-March 2009 until now, has been marked by signs of optimism in the face of still relatively negative macroeconomic and financial news.

The experiment in this chapter also selects portfolios of mutual funds in Egypt, in which the period from March 2000 to November 2001 is used on a weekly basis (83 weeks) in order to rank, select and construct portfolios, as detailed in the following sections. The subsequent 27-week period from December 2001 to June 2002 is then used to test the portfolios in terms of performance, and to compare them against each other and against the benchmark, which in this case is the EGX 30 index. These time periods are selected for the experiment in order to ensure the consistency of the utilised data. In particular, the Central Bank of Egypt (CBE, 2003, 2009) observes that during this period the activity of the emerging Egyptian financial market improved and the demand for mutual funds accelerated, as well as there being continuity in the trading rules adopted by the Egyptian stock exchange (Azmi, 2005).

The following figure illustrates the period covered by the study for both the British market (in a relatively volatile time) and the Egyptian market (in a relatively stable time).

In general, this chapter analyses certain portfolio-constructing methodologies using real data; therefore, any time period selected should not adversely impact the empirical part of this study.

Note that at the time of the experiment in Egypt, nineteen mutual funds existed in the stock exchange, while ten mutual funds are selected from UK's financial market based on the highest net asset value of index tracking funds and the availability of recent data. This chapter explores the issue of selecting five mutual funds in a portfolio, using the GP, Sharpe and Treynor methodologies.

Figure 4.1: Stock market performance from March 2000 through June 2009 in Britain and Egypt (the small boxes highlight the study periods of this chapter's experiments)

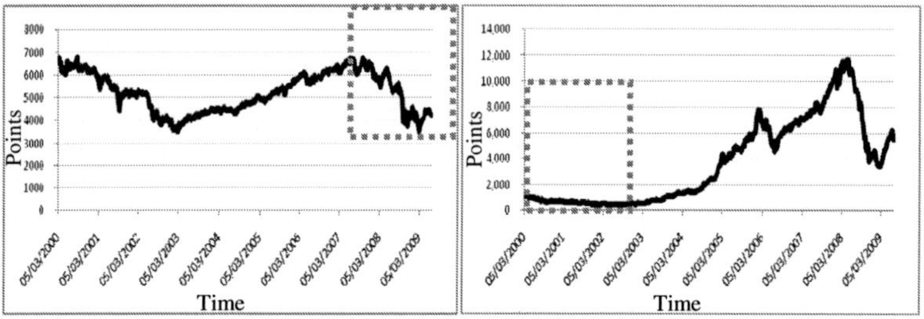

The British Stock Exchange Index (FTSE100)

The Egyptian Stock Exchange Index (EGX 30)

4.3 Goal Programming Applications to Mutual Fund Portfolio Selection

4.3.1 The Experiment in the UK's Financial Market

The Goal Programming methodology based on the Mean-Absolute Deviation model as proposed by Konno and Yamazaki (1991) is used in this chapter to select a portfolio from the ten studied mutual funds in UK's financial market as follows:

$$Min \sum_{t=1}^{88} (n_t + p_t) \qquad (4.1)$$

Subject to:

$$\sum_{j=1}^{10} (R_{jt} - I_t) X_j + n_t - p_t = 0 \qquad t = 1, \ldots, 88 \qquad (4.2)$$

$$\sum_{j=1}^{10} X_j = 1 \qquad (4.3)$$

$$X_j \geq 0 \quad j = 1, \ldots, 10 \quad n_t, p_t \geq 0 \quad t = 1, \ldots, 88$$

Where:

R_{jt}= Return of the jth mutual fund during period t.
I_t = Return of FTSE 100 during period t.
X_j= The proportion of the jth mutual fund selected.
n_t= The negative deviational variable for period t.
p_t = The positive deviational variable for period t.

All positive and negative deviational variables are penalised in the achievement function (4.1) with equal weights. The model contains 88 objective functions (4.2) belonging to the 88 time periods. The target value of zero for each objective function indicates that the difference between the index's performance and the portfolio's performance for each period should be the same, as an index tracking portfolio is sought. Constraint (4.3) ensures that the entire available fund is invested in the portfolio. Note that the normalisation techniques described in Jones and Tamiz (2010) are not used for the GP model in this chapter as all the objectives in (4.2) are measured with the same unit of measurement.

This model is designed so that the sum of deviations from the benchmark (index) is minimised. The following constraint (4.4) is added to ensure exactly 5 mutual funds are chosen for comparison with the portfolios selected by other methodologies:

$$x_j \leq 0.35 \qquad j = 1, \dots, 10 \qquad (4.4)$$

Note, in the above constraint 0.35 is a large enough value. However, for some problems it might be necessary to change this value in order to select the required number of mutual funds using the trial-and-error approach. Other modelling techniques such as a binary integer programming approach (Williams, 1978) may be required for a more elaborate approach.

4.3.2 The Experiment in Egypt's Financial Market

The Goal Programming methodology described in section 4.3.1 is used for the experiment in Egypt's mutual funds as follows:

$$Min \sum_{t=1}^{83} (n_t + p_t) \qquad (4.5)$$

Subject to:

$$\sum_{j=1}^{19}(R_{jt} - I_t)X_j + n_t - p_t = 0 \qquad t = 1, \dots, 83 \tag{4.6}$$

$$\sum_{j=1}^{19} X_j = 1 \tag{4.7}$$

$$X_j \geq 0 \qquad j = 1, \dots, 19 \qquad n_t, p_t \geq 0 \qquad t = 1, \dots, 83$$

Where:
I_t = Return of EGX 30 during period *t*.

The following constraint (4.8) is added to ensure exactly 5 funds are chosen:

$$x_j \leq 0.35 \qquad\qquad j = 1, \dots, 19 \tag{4.8}$$

For discussions on the choice of the right-hand side value, 0.35, see above.

4.3.3 Results

Using 880 observations for UK's experiment and 1,577 observations for Egypt's experiment in the constructing period, the following table shows the selected mutual funds in the GP portfolio and their proportions both in the UK and Egypt experiments (details of the mutual funds experimented are provided in table A-1, appendix A):

Table 4.1: GP Constructed Mutual Fund Portfolios in UK and Egypt

UK's Portfolio of Mutual Funds		Egypt's Portfolio of Mutual Funds	
Portfolio Constituents	Proportions (%)	Portfolio Constituents	Proportions (%)
AR	35.0	EA	35.0
GA	35.0	AE	34.2
AI	14.5	BA	17.2
JP	12.4	ED	8.00
FI	2.20	S1	5.60
Total proportions	100	Total proportions	100

4.4 Sharpe Applications for Mutual Fund Portfolio Selection

4.4.1 The Experiment in the UK's Financial Market

The ten British mutual funds are ranked based on the Sharpe Ratio (the higher the ratio, the better is the performance of the corresponding mutual fund).

The Sharpe Ratio is computed as follows:

$$S_j = \frac{R_j - BR}{SD_j} \qquad j = 1, \dots, 10$$

Where:

BR = Bank of England interest rate (represents the risk-free rate in England).

The best five mutual funds are selected to construct a portfolio of mutual funds. The constituents' proportions are assigned using weighting algorithm (3.2) in chapter 3 as follows:

$$X_i = \left[\frac{(R_i + C)}{5C + \sum_{i=1}^{5} R_i}\right] \times 100\%$$

4.4.2 The Experiment in Egypt's Financial Market

Nineteen mutual funds in the Egyptian stock exchange are ranked based on the Sharpe Ratio as follows:

$$S_j = \frac{R_j - ET}{SD_j} \qquad j = 1, \dots, 19$$

Where:

ET = 3-months Egyptian Treasury Bill yield (represents the risk-free rate in Egypt).

The best five mutual funds are selected to construct a portfolio of mutual funds. The constituents' proportions depend on each fund's return compared to the other selected mutual funds and they are computed using the weighting algorithm (3.2) in chapter three.

4.4.3 Results

Using the same number of observations as in GP experiments during the constructing period, the following table shows the selected mutual funds and their proportions in the Sharpe's portfolio in the UK and Egypt experiments:

Table 4.2: Sharpe's constructed Mutual Fund Portfolios in UK and Egypt

UK's Portfolio of Mutual Funds		Egypt's Portfolio of Mutual Funds	
The portfolio Constituents	Proportions (%)	The portfolio Constituents	Proportions (%)
HE	21.1	MI	15.5
AR	20.4	EG	20.8
SU	19.8	N1	17.9
JP	19.5	AE	22.6
AN	19.2	BC	23.2
Total proportions	100	Total proportions	100

4.5 Treynor Applications for Mutual Fund Portfolios Selection

4.5.1 The Experiment in the UK's Financial Market

The British mutual funds are ranked based on the Treynor ratio, which is computed as follows:

$$\mathrm{T}_j = \frac{\mathrm{R}_j - \mathrm{BR}}{Beta_j} \qquad j = 1, \ldots, 10$$

The best five mutual funds are selected with their portfolio proportions computed using weighting algorithm (3.2).

4.5.2 The Experiment in Egypt's Financial Market

The nineteen Egyptian mutual funds are ranked based on the Treynor ratio as follows:

$$T_j = \frac{R_j - ET}{Beta_j} \qquad j = 1, \ldots, 19$$

A portfolio of mutual funds is constructed using Treynor's ranking, where constituent funds' proportions are computed using weighting algorithm (3.2).

4.5.3 Results

The following table shows the selected mutual funds in Treynor's portfolio both in the UK (880 observations) and Egypt experiments (1,577 observations):

Table 4.3: Treynor's Constructed Mutual Fund Portfolios in UK and Egypt

UK Portfolio of Mutual Funds		Egypt Portfolio of Mutual Funds	
Portfolio Constituents	Proportions (%)	Portfolio Constituents	Proportions (%)
AR	27.1	MR	28.2
JP	28.3	ED	8.20
AN	22.1	N1	21.0
II	22.2	MI	18.2
SU	0.30	EG	24.4
Total proportions	100	Total proportions	100

4.6 Comparisons between the Selected Portfolios of Mutual Funds

4.6.1 Comparisons between the Mutual Fund Portfolios of the UK Experiment

Using 200 observations in the testing period, the following table shows the selected mutual funds in the three portfolios of the UK experiment, the portfolio return and risk:

Table 4.4: Sharpe's, Treynor's and GP's Constructed Portfolios in UK's Financial Market

Sharpe		Treynor		GP	
Portfolio constituents	Proportions (%)	Portfolio constituents	Proportions (%)	Portfolio constituents	Proportions (%)
HE	21.1	AR	27.1	AR	35.0
AR	20.4	JP	28.3	GA	35.0
SU	19.8	AN	22.1	AI	15.4
JP	19.5	II	22.2	JP	12.4
AN	19.2	SU	0.30	FI	2.20
Portfolio Return	0.005	Portfolio Return	0.003	Portfolio Return	0.003
Risk	0.033	Risk	0.040	Risk	0.034

The three portfolios of the British mutual funds are examined in terms of their returns during the testing period from February 2009 to June 2009.

The following figure depicts the returns on the Sharpe, Treynor and GP portfolios:

Figure 4.2: The returns for the constructed portfolios in UK's financial market

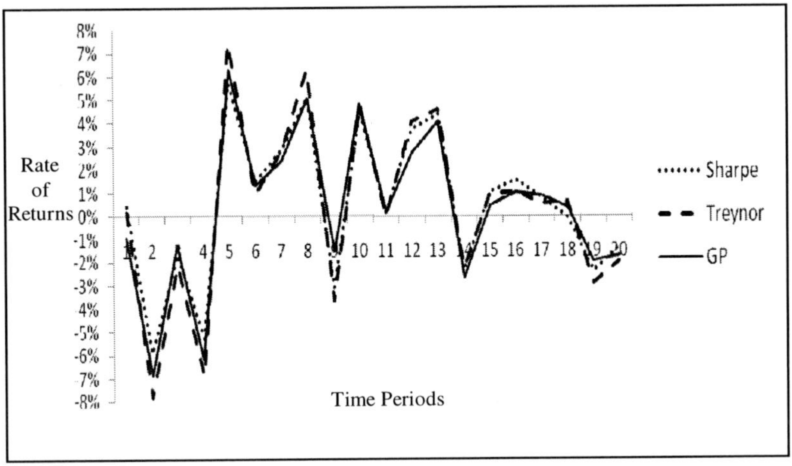

The deviations between the constructed portfolios, the sum of the absolute return deviations, are calculated as follows:

$$\sum_{t=1}^{20} |RS_t - RT_t| = 0.1214$$

$$\sum_{t=1}^{20} |RS_t - RGP_t| = 0.1094$$

$$\sum_{t=1}^{20} |RT_t - RGP_t| = 0.1381$$

Where:
RS_t = Return of Sharpe's portfolio.
RT_t = Return of Treynor's portfolio.
RGP_t = Return of GP's portfolio.

Accordingly, the least deviation is between Sharpe's portfolio and GP's portfolio, whereas the maximum deviation is between Treynor's and GP's portfolios.

The three portfolios are further compared to the benchmark as follows:

Figure 4.3: The returns for the constructed British portfolios vs. FTSE 100, the British financial market benchmark (BM)

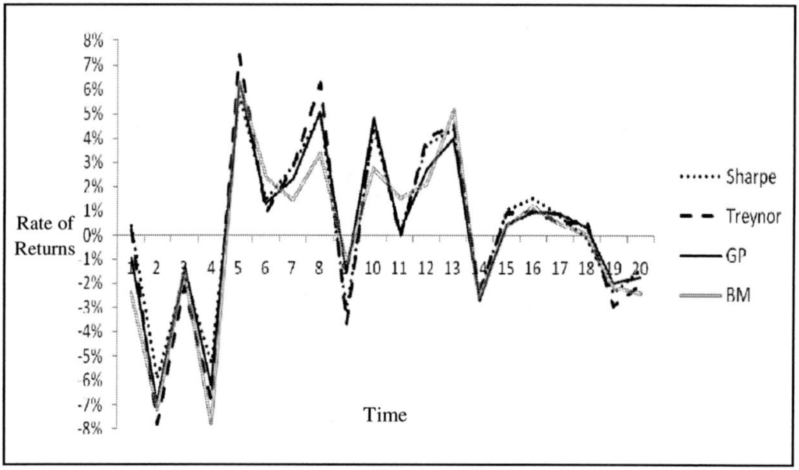

The tracking error, which measures the deviation of the portfolio's return compared to the market return, is calculated for the constructed portfolios as follows:

$$\sum_{t=1}^{20} |\mathrm{RS}_t - \mathrm{RBM}_t| = 0.2177$$

$$\sum_{t=1}^{20} |\mathrm{RT}_t - \mathrm{RBM}_t| = 0.2308$$

$$\sum_{t=1}^{20} |\mathrm{RGP}_t - \mathrm{RBM}_t| = 0.1487$$

Where:
RBM_t = Return of the benchmark.

Accordingly, the best portfolio, relative to the benchmark, is the portfolio constructed based on GP methodology, followed by the portfolio constructed based on Sharpe's methodology.

4.6.2 Comparisons between the Mutual Fund Portfolios of the Egyptian Experiment

Using 513 observations in the testing period, the following table shows the selected mutual funds in the three portfolios of the Egypt experiment:

Table 4.5: Sharpe's, Treynor's and GP's Constructed Portfolios in Egypt's Financial Market

Sharpe		Treynor		GP	
Portfolio constituents	Proportions (%)	Portfolio constituents	Proportions (%)	Portfolio constituents	Proportions (%)
MI	15.5	MR	28.2	EA	35.0
EG	20.8	ED	8.20	AE	34.2
N1	17.9	N1	21.0	BA	17.2
AE	22.6	MI	18.2	ED	8.00
BC	23.2	EG	24.4	S1	5.60
Portfolio Return	0.001	Portfolio Return	0.002	Portfolio Return	0.000
Risk	0.011	Risk	0.010	Risk	0.012

The three portfolios of the Egyptian mutual funds are examined in terms of their returns during the testing period from December 2001 to June 2002 (27 weekly returns).

The following figure depicts the returns on Sharpe, Treynor and GP portfolios:

Figure 4.4: The returns for the constructed Egyptian portfolios

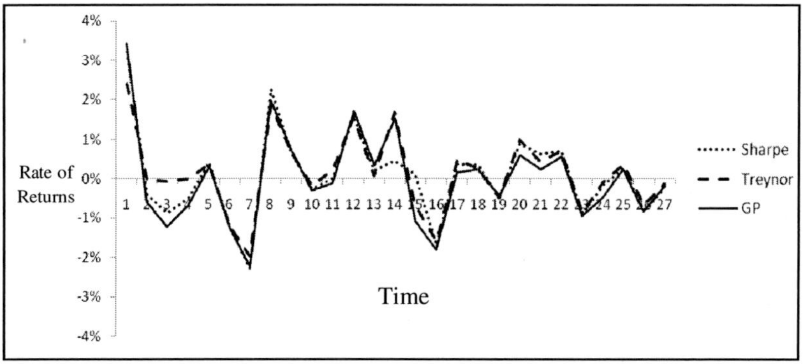

The sums of the absolute return deviations between the constructed portfolios are calculated as follows:

$$\sum_{t=1}^{27} |\mathrm{RS}_t - \mathrm{RT}_t| = 0.0678$$

$$\sum_{t=1}^{27} |\mathrm{RS}_t - \mathrm{RGP}_t| = 0.0604$$

$$\sum_{t=1}^{27} |\mathrm{RT}_t - \mathrm{RGP}_t| = 0.0758$$

Accordingly, the least deviation is between Sharpe's portfolio and GP's portfolio, whereas the maximum deviation is between Treynor's and GP's portfolios. A similar observation is reported in the UK experiment as well.

The three portfolios are further compared to the benchmark as in the following figure:

Figure 4.5: The returns for the constructed Egyptian portfolios vs. Egypt's financial market benchmark (BM)

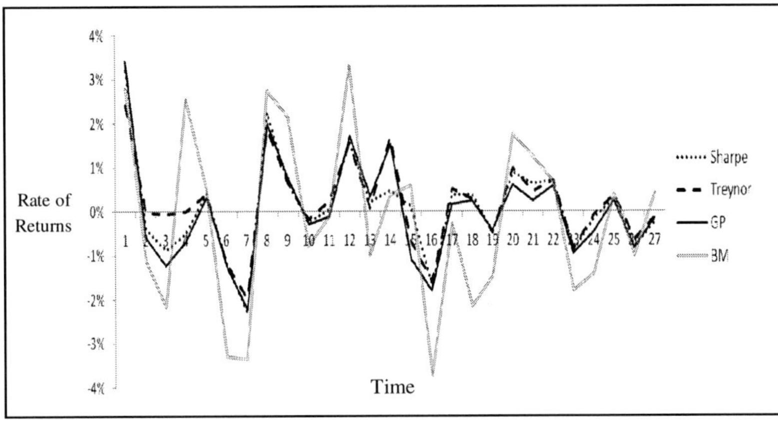

The tracking error is calculated as follows for the three portfolios, each compared to the benchmark:

$$\sum_{t=1}^{27} |RS_t - RBM_t| = 0.2579$$

$$\sum_{t=1}^{27} |RT_t - RBM_t| = 0.2956$$

$$\sum_{t=1}^{27} |RGP_t - RBM_t| = 0.2788$$

Accordingly, the best portfolio is the portfolio constructed based on Sharpe's ranking, followed by the portfolio constructed based on GP methodology.

4.7 Conclusion

Selection of portfolios of mutual funds both in the UK, a developed market, and in Egypt, an emerging market, has shown interesting results. This chapter offers three techniques for setting up portfolios of mutual funds. The performance comparison of the selected portfolios reveals that the portfolios constructed based on Sharpe and GP methodologies have the minimum deviations with each other as well as compared to the relevant benchmarks. Although the Sharpe and Treynor methodologies of ranking and selecting best mutual funds are well established historically, this chapter finds GP performing at least as good as both the Sharpe and Treynor methodologies, especially compared to the relevant benchmarks.

The results from the chapter suggest also that the GP methodology is as practical in a time of crisis (the experiment in UK's financial market recently) as in regular time (the experiment in Egypt's financial market nearly seven years ago). One of the reasons behind this success might be the fact that GP has an underlying satisficing philosophy (Romero, 1991), which could be more appealing for portfolio selection problems. This result is critical as the spread of the current credit crisis has challenged many of the key assumptions of modern finance, including the assumption of efficient markets and market allocations of risk.

Furthermore, there are two interesting results concerning the mutual funds studied and their benchmarks. First, the Egyptian benchmark shows lower variability (measured by the standard deviation, 0.02) compared to the British benchmark (0.04). This is somewhat to be expected since the data gathered for the British experiment was during a volatile time. Second, the deviation of the portfolio of the British mutual funds from its benchmark is much less than the Egyptian mutual funds' portfolio deviation from its benchmark. In other words, the British mutual funds portfolio seems to perform better than the Egyptian mutual funds portfolio relative to their respective benchmarks. This in part is due to the fact that the British mutual funds are index-trackers, whereas the Egyptian mutual funds are not clearly classified as index-trackers, or otherwise, in the Egyptian stock exchange.

The GP portfolio in the UK experiment is the best portfolio in terms of tracking the relevant benchmark, whereas the Sharpe portfolio is the best one in the Egypt experiment, followed by GP portfolio in terms of comparisons with the benchmark.

The GP model, in theory, should produce the lowest tracking error as it sets out to minimise the total deviations between the portfolio and the index. The experiments reported in Egypt's portfolios, however, do not seem to prove this point. Upon further investigation, it was deduced that:

- The reason why the tracking errors are so big is that some of the mutual funds are not classified as tracking funds, and as a consequence none of those models do a very good job of tracking the index.
- Some mutual funds constituents' are not necessarily from the stocks forming the Egyptian index at the time.

- And, from technical point of view, the GP model was designed to choose five mutual funds for the portfolio as the top five funds were selected by the Sharpe and Treynor models. Upon relaxing this rule (taking out constraint 4.8 in section 4.3.2) and re-running the model, the GP model selected only two funds to invest. Selecting the top two funds for Sharpe and Treynor and repeating the experiments produces the following tracking errors, with GP having the lowest:

Treynor	**Sharpe**	**GP**
0.286	0.223	0.211

Overall, the risk-return profiles of the portfolios produced by the various methodologies are close to each other with some variations (although GP is the closest portfolio to the relevant benchmark). This might be attributed to the fact that this chapter applies these methodologies to mutual funds where portfolio benefits are already supposed to be in place in terms of better risk-return tradeoffs. Accordingly, in the next chapter, further research is carried out with application to stocks using the same methodologies.

CHAPTER FIVE

PORTFOLIO SELECTION APPLICATIONS FOR STOCKS

5.1 Introduction

This chapter explores portfolio selection methodologies with ten stocks (part of the FTSE 100 at the time of the experiments, June 2009). The best five stocks are selected based on each methodology. The experiment includes a constructing period of 88 weeks (June 2007 to January 2009) with 880 observations, and a testing period of 20 weeks (from February 2009 to June 2009) with 200 observations (supplementary information about these stocks is given in table A-2, Appendix B).

5.2 Goal Programming Applications to Stock Portfolio Selection

The Goal Programming model for selecting five stocks is as follows:

$$Min \sum_{t=1}^{88} (n_t)$$

Subject to:

$$\sum_{j=1}^{10} (R_{jt} - I_t)X_j + n_t - p_t = 0 \qquad t = 1, \dots, 88$$

$$\sum_{j=1}^{10} X_j = 1$$

$$X_j \geq 0 \quad j = 1, \dots, 10 \quad n_t, p_t \geq 0 \quad t = 1, \dots, 88$$

Where:

I_t = Return of FTSE 100 during period *t*.

Notes:

- The five required stocks are selected without having to impose any extra restriction on the model. If it did not select the required number, then a constraint similar to (4.4) in chapter four would have to be imposed.
- The other methodologies used in this chapter, namely Sharpe and Treynor, select portfolios while considering risk and return. For comparison purposes in the GP model risk is represented by the relevant index and return is maximised by penalising the negative deviational variables in the achievement function.
- The model aims to select active portfolios, while keeping the risk close to the index. This is imposed by setting the target values to zero in the objective functions and penalising the negative deviational variables in the achievement function.

The following table shows the selected stocks in GP's portfolio:

Table 5.1: GP's Stocks Portfolio

Portfolio of Stocks	HS	BH	GS	PE	UN	Average Return
Proportions (%)	25.97	23.50	22.21	17.63	10.69	-0.09

5.3 Sharpe Applications for Stock Portfolio Selection

The ten stocks in the UK stock exchange are ranked based on the Sharpe Ratio (the higher the ratio, the better is the performance of the corresponding stock in terms of risk-adjusted return).

The Sharpe Ratio is computed as follows for the ten stocks:

$$S_j = \frac{R_j - BR}{SD_j} \qquad j = 1, \ldots, 10$$

Where:
BR = Bank of England interest rate (the risk-free rate).

The following table shows the Sharpe ratio for each of the ten stocks.

Table 5.2: The Sharpe ratio for the 10 stocks and their ranking

Stock Name	TR	LB	RT	BH	RD	VO	HS	UN	GS	PE
Sharpe Ratio	**0.05**	**-0.42**	**-0.44**	**-0.46**	**-0.87**	**-0.92**	**-1.06**	**-1.08**	**-1.09**	**-1.13**
Sharpe Ranking 1 = best 10 = worst	**1**	**2**	**3**	**4**	**5**	**6**	**7**	**8**	**9**	**10**

The top five stocks are selected to construct the portfolio. The constituent's stock proportion depends on each stock's Sharpe ratio. The portfolio proportions are computed using the weighting algorithms of section 3.7 in chapter three. Accordingly, the following table shows the top five stocks and their proportions in Sharpe's stock portfolio:

Table 5.3: Sharpe's Stocks Portfolio

Portfolio of Stocks	TR	LB	RT	BH	RD	Average Return
Proportions (%)	41.06	20.48	19.49	18.70	0.26	0.87

5.4 Treynor Applications for Stock Portfolio Selection

The ten stocks are ranked based on the Treynor Ratio (the higher the ratio, the better is the performance of the corresponding stock).

The Treynor Ratio is computed as follows for the ten stocks:

$$T_j = \frac{R_j - BR}{Beta_j} \qquad j = 1, \dots, 10$$

The following table shows the Treynor ratio for each of the ten stocks.

Table 5.4: The Treynor ratio for the 10 stocks and their ranking

Stock Name	TR	BH	LB	RT	RD	VO	HS	GS	PE	UN
Treynor Ratio	**0.05**	**-0.02**	**-0.03**	**-0.03**	**-0.05**	**-0.06**	**-0.06**	**-0.08**	**-0.08**	**-0.09**
Treynor Ranking 1 = best 10 = worst	**1**	**2**	**3**	**4**	**5**	**6**	**7**	**8**	**9**	**10**

The top five stocks are selected to construct a portfolio of stocks. The constituent's stock proportions depend on each stock's Treynor ratio. The portfolio proportions are computed using the weighting algorithms of section 3.7. Accordingly, the following table shows the top five stocks and their proportions in the Treynor's stock portfolio:

Table 5.5: Treynor's Stocks Portfolio

Portfolio of Stocks	TR	BH	LB	RT	RD	Average Return
Proportions (%)	23.00	19.67	19.30	19.29	18.74	0.63

5.5 Comparison between the Selected Stock Portfolios

The three stock portfolios are examined in terms of their returns during the testing period from February 2009 to June 2009 (20 weeks).

The following figure depicts the returns on the GP, Sharpe and Treynor portfolios:

Figure 5.1: The returns for the constructed stock portfolios

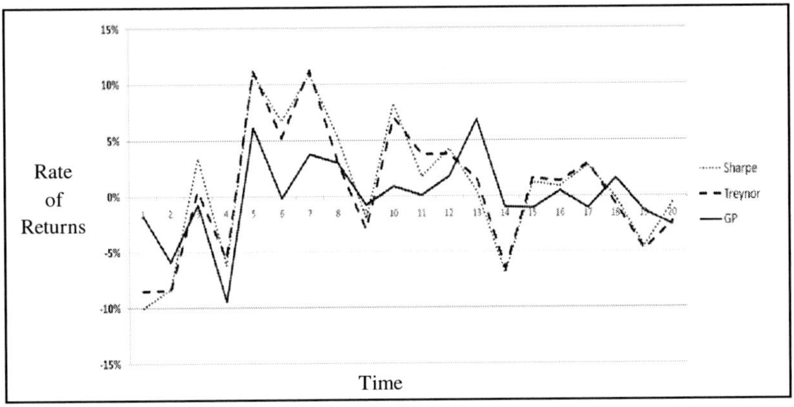

The deviations between the constructed portfolios, the sum of the absolute return deviations, are calculated as follows:

$$\sum_{t=1}^{20} |RS_t - RT_t| = 0.190$$

$$\sum_{t=1}^{20} |RS_t - RGP_t| = 0.711$$

$$\sum_{t=1}^{20} |RT_t - RGP_t| = 0.635$$

Accordingly, the least deviation is between Sharpe's portfolio and Treynor's portfolio, whereas the maximum deviation is between Sharpe's and GP's portfolios.

The three portfolios are further compared to the benchmark as follows:

Figure 5.2: The returns for the constructed stock portfolios vs. FTSE 100, the British financial market benchmark (BM)

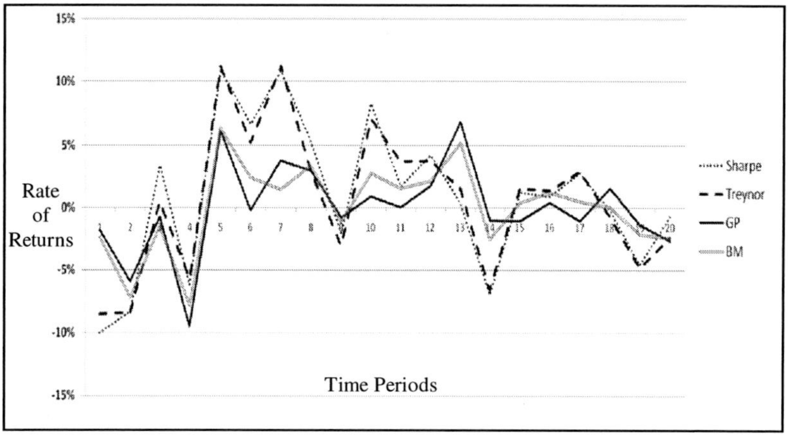

The tracking error, which measures the deviation of the portfolio's return compared to the market return, is calculated for the constructed portfolios as follows:

$$\sum_{t=1}^{20} |\mathrm{RS}_t - \mathrm{RBM}_t| = 0.580$$

$$\sum_{t=1}^{20} |\mathrm{RT}_t - \mathrm{RBM}_t| = 0.531$$

$$\sum_{t=1}^{20} |\mathrm{RGP}_t - \mathrm{RBM}_t| = 0.212$$

Accordingly, the best portfolio, relative to the benchmark, is the portfolio constructed based on GP methodology, followed by the portfolio constructed based on Treynor's methodology.

5.6 Conclusion

This chapter explores selecting stock portfolios with GP, Sharpe and Treynor methods.

The performance comparison between the three portfolios reveals that the portfolio constructed based on Goal Programming has the minimum deviation relative to the benchmark, as the GP model was designed to have the same level of risk as the index. At the same time, GP stock portfolio has the lowest average return amongst other portfolios.

Although both Sharpe and Treynor stock portfolios have higher average returns compared to the GP portfolio, these returns are accompanied by high risks as follows:

The Portfolios	GP	Sharpe	Treynor
Average return	-0.09%	0.87%	0.63%
Total Risk	0.037	0.060	0.057

These various risk-return combinations could be considered as different points in the efficient frontier, in which selecting the best one would depend on the decision maker's tolerance to risk and preferences for a corresponding return.

GP methodology is reasonable in keeping the portfolio attributes close to the relevant benchmark and hence avoids excessive risk which is naturally accompanied by lower return.

CHAPTER SIX

INVESTMENT WEIGHTING SCHEMES FOR PORTFOLIOS

6.1 Introduction

Portfolio analysis theory implies that an investor's problem includes security analysis, portfolio analysis and portfolio selection. Even after completing those three investment tasks, the investor is sometimes required to perform one more key task, which is deciding on the use of appropriate weighting schemes for selecting portfolio proportions. Therefore, weighting schemes could be considered as an integral part of portfolio selection problems.

In fact, the proportion that is assigned to a given asset (stock or mutual fund) in a portfolio can make a contribution to return that is just as important as the asset selection and investment timing decisions (Block and French, 2002). There are almost as many weighting schemes as there are portfolio constituents. This chapter explores several schemes for obtaining portfolio proportions. The schemes to be investigated are as follows: equal and ranking weights, Sharpe, Treynor, return-based weightings, Markowitz, and Goal Programming.

The experiments reported in this chapter are concerned with selecting a number of assets (stocks or mutual funds), say five, from a set of assets, say ten, based on various criteria to be described in later sections. The weighting schemes are then applied to find the proportion of the fund to be invested in each of the five assets (details of the experimented stocks and mutual funds in this chapter are provided in table A-3, appendix C).

6.2 Weighting Schemes for Mutual Fund Portfolios

Once a decision maker decides on the quality and quantity of assets to be included in his/her portfolio, the choice of an appropriate weighting scheme to establish the proportions of the mutual fund in the portfolio is the next important decision.

In this chapter, the top five mutual funds out of ten from UK's financial market are selected based on the Sharpe ratio. The following table shows the ten mutual funds, their Sharpe ratio and their ranking:

Table 6.1: The 10 mutual funds and their Sharpe ranking

Mutual Fund Name	HE	AR	SU	JP	AN	FC	II	GA	FI	AI
Sharpe Ratio	**-1.33**	**-1.38**	**-1.41**	**-1.43**	**-1.46**	**-1.48**	**-1.48**	**-1.67**	**-1.67**	**-1.68**
Sharpe Ranking 1 = best 10 = worst	**1**	**2**	**3**	**4**	**5**	**6**	**7**	**8**	**9**	**10**

The top five mutual funds (ranked 1 to 5 in table 6.1) are used throughout section 6.2 to investigate the portfolio's performance using different weighting schemes during the time period starting from 6 February 2009 to 26 June 2009 on a weekly basis. The experiments have a total of 105 observations for 21 weeks ($t = 1, \ldots, 21$).

6.2.1 Equal Weight

The proportion for each constituent for the equal weight scheme, which is the simplest weighting scheme, is as follows:

$$X_j = 20\% \qquad j = 1, \ldots, 5$$

6.2.2 Sharpe Weight

The Sharpe Ratio is calculated for the five mutual funds as follows:

$$S_j = \frac{R_j - BR}{SD_j} \qquad j = 1, \ldots, 5 \qquad (6.1)$$

Where:

BR = Bank of England interest rate.

The Sharpe ratios for the selected mutual funds are shown in the following table:

Table 6.2: The Sharpe ratios for the 5 mutual funds

S_j $j = 1, \ldots, 5$	S_1	S_2	S_3	S_4	S_5
Mutual Funds Name	HE	AR	SU	JP	AN
Sharpe Ratio	-1.33	-1.38	-1.41	-1.43	-1.46

Using weighting algorithm 2 (section 3.7, chapter three), the following portfolio proportions are obtained:

Table 6.3: The Sharpe proportions for the 5 mutual funds

X_j $j = 1, \ldots, 5$	X_1	X_2	X_3	X_4	X_5
Mutual Funds Name	HE	AR	SU	JP	AN
Sharpe Proportions (%)	21.06	20.33	19.89	19.57	19.16

6.2.3 Treynor Weight

The Treynor Ratio is calculated for the five mutual funds as follows:

$$T_j = \frac{R_j - BR}{Beta_j} \qquad j = 1, \ldots, 5 \tag{6.2}$$

The Treynor ratios for the selected mutual funds are shown in the following table:

Table 6.4: The Treynor ratios for the 5 mutual funds

T_j $j = 1, \ldots, 5$	T_1	T_2	T_3	T_4	T_5
Mutual Funds Name	HE	AR	SU	JP	AN
Treynor Ratio	-0.076	-0.067	-0.074	-0.069	-0.072

Using weighting algorithm 2, the following portfolio proportions are obtained:

Table 6.5: The Treynor proportions for the 5 mutual funds

X_j $j = 1, \dots, 5$	X_1	X_2	X_3	X_4	X_5
Mutual Funds Name	HE	AR	SU	JP	AN
Treynor Proportions (%)	18.89	21.40	19.34	20.53	19.84

6.2.4 Returns Weight

The average rate of return during the period for each of the selected mutual funds is shown in the following table:

Table 6.6: The average rate of return for the 5 mutual funds

R_j $j = 1, \dots, 5$	R_1	R_2	R_3	R_4	R_5
Mutual Funds Name	HE	AR	SU	JP	AN
Average Return (%)	-0.90	-0.48	-0.77	-0.44	-0.53

Using weighting algorithm 2, the following portfolio proportions are obtained:

Table 6.7: The return proportions for the 5 mutual funds

X_j $j = 1, \dots, 5$	X_1	X_2	X_3	X_4	X_5
Mutual Funds Name	HE	AR	SU	JP	AN
Return Proportions (%)	12.81	24.17	15.04	26.17	21.80

6.2.5 Ranking Weight

The Ranking weight is one of the simplest weighting schemes, wherein each asset in a portfolio is given a proportion based on its ranking according to any ranking method (i.e., if there are five assets in a portfolio, the asset with a rank of one gets the highest proportion, whereas the asset with a rank of five gets the lowest proportion).

The ranking proportions for the five mutual funds are shown in table 6.8. The jth proportion is calculated by $\frac{6-j}{15}$ (where 15=5+4+3+2+1).

Table 6.8: The ranking proportions for the 5 mutual funds

$X_j \quad j = 1, \ldots, 5$	X_1	X_2	X_3	X_4	X_5
Mutual Funds Name	HE	AR	SU	JP	AN
Ranking Proportions (%)	$\frac{5}{15} =$ 33.33	$\frac{4}{15} =$ 26.67	$\frac{3}{15} =$ 20.00	$\frac{2}{15} =$ 13.33	$\frac{1}{15} =$ 6.67

6.2.6 GP Weight

Two GP models are proposed for selecting the proportions of each mutual fund in the portfolio; one for comparison with other portfolios, called GPMF1, and the second for comparison with the benchmark, called GPMF2. In both models the values for X_j (the proportions) are restricted to take a value of at least 15% so that all five mutual funds are selected for comparison purposes.

The GPMF1 model for the five mutual funds is as follows:

$$Min \sum_{t=1}^{21} (n_t)$$

Subject to:

$$\sum_{j=1}^{5} R_{jt} X_j + n_t - p_t = 0.05 \qquad t = 1, \ldots, 21$$

$$\sum_{j=1}^{5} X_j = 1$$

$$X_j \geq 0.15 \qquad j = 1, \ldots, 5 \qquad n_t, p_t \geq 0 \qquad t = 1, \ldots, 21$$

This model is set up to maximise the portfolio's return. The target values are all set at 5%, which is considered a realistic return for mutual funds in the testing period. Note that there is no need for the use of the normalisation methods described in chapter three (Tamiz and Jones, 1997) as all the target values are the same and measured in the same unit of measurement.

The following table shows the GP proportions for the five mutual funds.

Table 6.9: The GPMF1 proportions for the 5 mutual funds

$X_j \quad j = 1, \dots, 5$	X_1	X_2	X_3	X_4	X_5
Mutual Funds Name	HE	AR	SU	JP	AN
GPMF1 Proportions (%)	40.00	15.00	15.00	15.00	15.00

The GPMF2 model for the five mutual funds based on Konno's model and its results are as follows:

$$Min \sum_{t=1}^{21} (n_t + p_t)$$

Subject to:

$$\sum_{j=1}^{5} (R_{jt} - I_t)X_j + n_t - p_t = 0 \qquad t = 1, \dots, 21$$

$$\sum_{j=1}^{5} X_j = 1$$

$$X_j \geq 0.15 \qquad j = 1, \dots, 5 \qquad n_t, p_t \geq 0 \qquad t = 1, \dots, 21$$

Table 6.10: The GPMF2 proportions for the 5 mutual funds

$X_j \quad j = 1, \dots, 5$	X_1	X_2	X_3	X_4	X_5
Mutual Funds Name	HE	AR	SU	JP	AN
GPMF2 Proportions (%)	15.00	15.00	15.00	40.00	15.00

6.2.7 Markowitz Weight

The Markowitz model is as follows:

$$Min \sum_{i=1}^{5}\sum_{j=1}^{5} x_i \sigma_{ij} x_j$$

Subject to:

$$\sum\nolimits_{j=1}^{5} R_j X_j \geq \overline{I_t}$$

$$\sum_{j=1}^{5} X_j = 1$$

$$X_j \geq 0.15 \quad j = 1, \dots, 5$$

Where:
$\overline{I_t}$ is the average return of the benchmark (FTSE 100) during the period.

The following table shows the Markowitz proportions for the five mutual funds.

Table 6.11: The Markowitz proportions for the 5 mutual funds

$X_j \quad j = 1, \dots, 5$	X_1	X_2	X_3	X_4	X_5
Mutual Funds Name	HE	AR	SU	JP	AN
Markowitz Proportions (%)	40.00	15.00	15.00	15.00	15.00

6.2.8 Comparison between the Weighting Schemes for Mutual Fund Portfolios

The following table compares the various weighting schemes based on their portfolios' average return and total risk.

Table 6.12: The average return and total risk of portfolios based on various weighting schemes

Portfolio constituents	Weighting Schemes (%)						
	Equal Weight	Sharpe Weight	Treynor Weight	Return Weight	Ranking Weight	GPMF1 Weight	Markowitz Weight
HE	20.00	21.06	18.89	0.54	33.33	40.00	40.00
AR	20.00	20.33	21.40	30.21	26.67	15.00	15.00
SU	20.00	19.89	19.43	9.90	20.00	15.00	15.00
JP	20.00	19.57	20.53	32.76	13.33	15.00	15.00
AN	20.00	19.16	19.84	26.58	6.67	15.00	15.00
Average Portfolio Return	0.56	0.57	0.55	0.48	0.72	0.77	0.77
Total Risk	0.0329	0.0327	0.0333	0.0383	0.0306	0.0292	0.0292
Sharpe Ratio	15.6	16.0	15.1	11.3	22.0	24.7	24.7

As shown in the table, return and risk are used to compare portfolios against each other. The risk is measured by the standard deviation measuring how much the return on a portfolio deviates from the average returns.

Table 6.12 illustrates that both the GPMF1-weighted portfolio and the Markowitz-weighted portfolio are the ones with the highest rate of return compared to other portfolios, and moreover they are the two portfolios that have the lowest risk level amongst all other portfolios.

The table also shows that the return-based portfolio has the lowest return which is associated with the highest risk.

When comparing average returns with total risks for all portfolios, the GPMF1-weighted portfolio and the Markowitz-weighted portfolio provide the best compromise between risk and return. The Sharpe ratio is used to establish whether the investor's return is due to smart investing decisions or the result of excess risk.

The following table compares the portfolios with their benchmark using the tracking error (TE).

Table 6.13: The tracking error of the portfolios based on various weighting schemes

Portfolio Constituents	Weighting Schemes (%)						
	Equal Weight	Sharpe Weight	Treynor Weight	Return Weight	Ranking Weight	GPMF2 Weight	Markowitz Weight
Average Portfolio Return	0.56	0.57	0.55	0.48	0.72	0.49	0.77
Average Benchmark Return	0.16	0.16	0.16	0.16	0.16	0.16	0.16
Tracking Error	0.2147	0.2159	0.2137	0.2076	0.2314	0.2092	0.2395

If the investment goal is to keep track of a relevant benchmark (so as to avoid excessive risk), the best portfolio to select is the one that has the lowest tracking error. Table 6.13 shows that the return-weighted portfolio is the best portfolio in tracking the benchmark with a tracking error of 0.2076 and a return of 0.48, followed by the GPMF2-weighted portfolio with a tracking error of 0.2092 and a return of 0.49 (higher than the return-weighted portfolio's return).

6.3 Weighting Schemes for Stock Portfolios

In this section, the top five stocks out of ten (from FTSE 100 constituents) are selected based on their P/E ratio. The following table shows the ten stocks, their P/E and their ranking:

Table 6.14: The 10 stocks ranked based on their P/E ratio

Stock name	HS	TR	PE	BH	UN	RT	RD	VO	GS	LB
P/E	**158.1**	**19.7**	**18.3**	**18.2**	**17.9**	**17.3**	**13.4**	**12.8**	**11.4**	**1.7**
P/E Ranking 1 = best 10 = worst	1	2	3	4	5	6	7	8	9	10

The top five stocks (ranked 1 to 5 in table 6.14) are used throughout section 6.3 for investigating their portfolio's performance using different weighting schemes during the time period from 6 February 2009 to 26 June 2009 on a weekly basis. The experiments have a total of 105 observations for 21 weeks ($t = 1, \dots, 21$).

6.3.1 Equal Weight

The proportion for each stock in the equal weight portfolio is as follows:

$$X_j = 20\% \qquad\qquad j = 1, \dots, 5$$

6.3.2 Sharpe Weight

The Sharpe Ratio is calculated for the five stocks (using equation 6.1) in order to measure the units of return compared to the units of risk (measured by the standard deviation).

The following table shows the values of the Sharpe ratio for each of the five stocks:

Table 6.15: The Sharpe ratios for the 5 stocks

$S_j \quad j = 1, \dots, 5$	S_1	S_2	S_3	S_4	S_5
Stock Name	HS	TR	PE	BH	UN
Sharpe Ratio	-1.07	0.05	-1.14	-0.48	-1.08

Using weighting algorithm 3.2, the following portfolio proportions are obtained:

Table 6.16: The Sharpe proportions for the 5 stocks

$X_j \quad j = 1, \dots, 5$	X_1	X_2	X_3	X_4	X_5
Stock Name	HS	TR	PE	BH	UN
Sharpe Proportions (%)	3.69	59.90	0.16	33.32	2.93

6.3.3 Treynor Weight

The Treynor Ratio is calculated for the five stocks (using equation 6.2) in order to measure the units of return compared to the units of risk (measured by the Beta Coefficient).

The Treynor ratios for the selected stocks are shown in the following table:

Table 6.17: The Treynor ratios for the 5 stocks

$T_j \quad j = 1, \dots, 5$	T_1	T_2	T_3	T_4	T_5
Stock Name	HS	TR	PE	BH	UN
Treynor Ratio	-0.061	0.050	-0.078	-0.025	-0.082

Using weighting algorithm 3.2, the following portfolio proportions are obtained:

Table 6.18: The Treynor proportions for the 5 stocks

$X_j \quad j = 1, \dots, 5$	X_1	X_2	X_3	X_4	X_5
Stock Name	HS	TR	PE	BH	UN
Treynor Proportions (%)	19.45	22.29	19.00	20.35	18.91

6.3.4 Returns Weight

The average rate of return during the period for each of the selected stocks is shown in the following table:

Table 6.19: The average rate of return for the 5 stocks

$R_j \quad j = 1, \dots, 5$	R_1	R_2	R_3	R_4	R_5
Stock Name	HS	TR	PE	BH	UN
Average Return	-0.005	0.096	-0.003	0.003	0.001

Using weighting algorithm 3.2, the following portfolio proportions are obtained:

Table 6.20: The return proportions for the 5 stocks

$X_j \quad j = 1, \dots, 5$	X_1	X_2	X_3	X_4	X_5
Stock Name	HS	TR	PE	BH	UN
Return Proportions (%)	15.91	33.51	16.33	17.35	16.90

6.3.5 Ranking Weight

The ranking weights for the five stocks are shown in table 6.21. The jth ranking ratio is calculated by $\frac{6-j}{15}$ (where 15=5+4+3+2+1).

Table 6.21: The ranking proportion for the 5 stocks

$X_j \quad j = 1, \dots, 5$	X_1	X_2	X_3	X_4	X_5
Stock Name	HS	TR	PE	BH	UN
Ranking Proportions (%)	$\frac{5}{15} =$ 33.33	$\frac{4}{15} =$ 26.67	$\frac{3}{15} =$ 20.00	$\frac{2}{15} =$ 13.33	$\frac{1}{15} =$ 6.67

6.3.6 GP Weight

Two GP models are proposed for selecting the proportions of each stock in the portfolio. The GPS1 model is for comparison with other portfolios, while GPS2 is for comparison with the benchmark.

The GPS1 model for the five stocks is as follows:

$$Min \sum_{t=1}^{21} (n_t)$$

Subject to:

$$\sum_{j=1}^{5} R_{jt} X_j + n_t - p_t = 0.10 \qquad t = 1, \dots, 21$$

$$\sum_{j=1}^{5} X_j = 1$$

$$X_j \geq 0.15 \quad j = 1, \ldots, 5 \quad n_t, p_t \geq 0 \quad t = 1, \ldots, 21$$

The following table shows the GPS1 proportions for the five stocks.

Table 6.22: The GPS1 proportions for the 5 stocks

$X_j \quad j = 1, \ldots, 5$	X_1	X_2	X_3	X_4	X_5
Stock Name	HS	TR	PE	BH	UN
GPS1 Proportions (%)	15.00	40.00	15.00	15.00	15.00

The GPS2 model for the five stocks is as follows (the GPS2 model is maximising return relative to index for the five stocks):

$$Min \sum_{t=1}^{21} (n_t)$$

Subject to:

$$\sum_{j=1}^{5} (R_{jt} - I_t)X_j + n_t - p_t = 0 \quad t = 1, \ldots, 21$$

$$\sum_{j=1}^{5} X_j = 1$$

$$X_j \geq 0 \quad j = 1, \ldots, 5 \quad n_t, p_t \geq 0 \quad t = 1, \ldots, 21$$

Note, in GPS2 all the five stocks are selected without having to impose any extra restriction on the model.

The following table shows the GPS2 proportions for the five stocks:

Table 6.23: The GPS2 proportions for the 5 stocks

$X_j \quad j = 1, \ldots, 5$	X_1	X_2	X_3	X_4	X_5
Stock Name	HS	TR	PE	BH	UN
GPS2 Proportions (%)	16.27	38.99	21.21	4.70	18.82

6.3.7 Markowitz Weight

The Markowitz model is computed (using a similar Markowitz model as in section 6.2.7), but this time with application to stocks.

The following table shows the Markowitz proportions for the five stocks.

Table 6.24: The Markowitz proportions for the 5 stocks

$X_j \quad j = 1, \dots, 5$	X_1	X_2	X_3	X_4	X_5
Stock Name	HS	TR	PE	BH	UN
Markowitz Proportions (%)	15.00	15.00	29.50	15.00	25.50

6.3.8 Market Cap Weight

The market capitalisation for each of the selected stocks is shown in the following table:

Table 6.25: The market capitalisation proportions for the 5 stocks

Stock Name	HS	TR	PE	BH	UN
Market Capitalisation (Billions of GBP)	123.84	19.40	8.02	134.42	61.08

Using weighting algorithm 1, the following portfolio proportions are obtained:

Table 6.26: The market cap proportions for the 5 stocks

$X_j \quad j = 1, \dots, 5$	X_1	X_2	X_3	X_4	X_5
Stock Name	HS	TR	PE	BH	UN
Market Cap Proportions (%)	35.71	5.60	2.31	38.76	17.62

6.3.9 Comparison between the Weighting Schemes for Stock Portfolios

The following table compares the various weighting schemes based on their portfolios' average return, total risk and Sharpe ratio.

Table 6.27: The average return, total risk and Sharpe ratio of portfolios based on various weighting schemes

Portfolio constituents	Weighting Schemes (%)							
	Equal Weight	Sharpe Weight	Treynor Weight	Return Weight	Ranking Weight	GPS1 Weight	Markowitz Weight	Market Cap Weight
HS	20.00	3.69	19.45	15.91	33.33	16.27	15.00	35.71
TR	20.00	59.90	22.29	33.51	26.67	38.99	15.00	5.60
PE	20.00	0.16	19.00	16.33	20.00	21.21	29.50	2.31
BH	20.00	33.32	20.35	17.35	13.33	4.70	15.00	38.76
UN	20.00	2.93	18.91	16.90	6.67	18.82	25.50	17.62
Average Portfolio Return	0.45	0.97	0.48	0.56	0.59	0.61	0.26	0.65
Total Risk	0.039	0.044	0.039	0.038	0.047	0.038	0.034	0.053
Sharpe Ratio	10.3	20.9	11.1	13.5	11.5	14.8	6.2	11.4

Table 6.27 shows return, risk and Sharpe ratio for all portfolios, in which the Sharpe-weighted portfolio is the one with the highest rate of return compared to other portfolios, whereas the Markowitz-weighted portfolio has the lowest return.

However, the Markowitz-weighted portfolio is the one with the lowest total risk compared to other portfolios, whereas the Market Cap–weighted portfolio has the highest risk.

When comparing average returns with total risks for all portfolios, the Sharpe-weighted portfolio provides the best compromise between risk and return, followed by the GP-weighted portfolio. The Sharpe ratio is used to establish whether the investor's return is due to sound investing decisions or the result of excess risk.

The following table compares the portfolios with their benchmark using the tracking error.

Table 6.28: The tracking error of the portfolios based on various weighting schemes

Portfolio Constituents	Weighting Schemes (%)							
	Equal Weight	Sharpe Weight	Treynor Weight	Return Weight	Ranking Weight	GPS2 Weight	Markowitz Weight	Market Cap Weight
Average Portfolio Return	0.45	0.97	0.48	0.56	0.59	0.49	0.26	0.65
Average Benchmark Return	0.16	0.16	0.16	0.16	0.16	0.16	0.16	0.16
Tracking Error	0.197	0.390	0.197	0.200	0.262	0.183	0.212	0.331

If the investment goal is to keep track of a relevant benchmark, the best portfolio would be the one that has the lowest tracking error with the relevant benchmark. Table 6.28 shows that the GP-weighted portfolio is the best portfolio in tracking the benchmark, with a tracking error of 0.183, followed by the Treynor-weighted portfolio and, surprisingly, the equal weight portfolio (albeit that the GPS2-weighted and Treynor-weighted portfolios have a higher return compared to the equal weight portfolio).

6.4 Conclusion

This chapter explores several weighting schemes for selecting portfolio proportions. Applications to mutual funds and stocks are investigated in distinguishable experiments in order to make meaningful comparisons and in an attempt to validate the results using different assets. The weighting schemes comparisons show that using an optimisation methodology produces more reasonable portfolio weights when considering both risk and return. This is particularly true for weighting schemes in mutual fund portfolios, where GP and Markowitz weighting schemes achieve the best return and risk compared to other portfolios.

However, in the experiments on weighting schemes in stock portfolios, the Sharpe and GP weighting schemes achieve the best results compared to other portfolios. The equal weight scheme produces the same level of tracking error as that achieved by the Treynor-weighted portfolio, but with less return.

Overall, the best weighting schemes in mutual funds experiments, in terms of risk-adjusted returns for resulting portfolios, are the GP and Markowitz weighting schemes (with a Sharpe ratio of 24.7 for each of them), followed by the Ranking and Sharpe weights (with Sharpe ratios of 22 and 16, respectively). However, when comparing the resulting portfolios with the relevant benchmark, the Return and GP weights are the best with the lowest tracking errors of 0.208 and 0.209 respectively, followed by Treynor and Equal Weight.

The results of weighting schemes with applications to stocks imply that the Sharpe and GP weighting schemes are the best compared to others in terms of risk-adjusted returns, followed by Return and Ranking weights. GP is further the weighting scheme with the lowest TE of 0.183, followed by Treynor and Equal Weight (each with a TE of 0.197), and then by Return and Markowitz weights.

In this chapter the Sharpe ratio is used to select the initial five mutual funds and the P/E ratios are used to select the initial five stocks. The weighting schemes are subsequently applied to calculate the respective proportions in each portfolio. Clearly future research is warranted on these or similar weighting schemes based on other selection criteria for the initial assets.

Finally, this chapter provides many choices of weighting schemes for investors to explore in order to establish the preferred proportions for investment portfolios. From an academic point of view, it is hoped that some of the weighting schemes experimented with in this chapter will assist in stimulating further research and innovation in obtaining systematic ways for deciding on portfolio constituents' proportions.

CHAPTER SEVEN

MULTIPLE CRITERIA INVESTMENT PORTFOLIO SELECTION USING GOAL PROGRAMMING MODELS

7.1 Introduction and Background

In finance, a fundamental principle is to determine the relationship between expected return and risk when markets are in equilibrium. The Capital Asset Pricing Model (CAPM) and the Arbitrage Pricing Theory (APT) are two foundations for computing the trade-off between risk and return (Vardavaki and Mylonakis, 2007).

The CAPM (Sharpe, 1964) holds that only one type of systematic risk (the market risk) influences expected security return; whereas a multi-factor model such as APT (Ross, 1976) suggests that a variety of economic sources of risk (GDP, inflation, interest rate, etc.) influence the return. Multifactor (Fama and French, 1993; Fama, 1996) extensions of CAPM, however, associate return not only with market risk, but also with other risk factors such as size and book-to-market equity (the sources of common risk factors in returns).

The CAPM model is based on very strong theoretical assumptions which are not entirely respected by markets in practice. The modified versions of the CAPM only provide partial solutions. Theorists thus sought to develop a more general model, while at the same time simplifying the assumptions. The result was a family of models that were referred to collectively as multi-factor models. These models constitute an alternative theory to the CAPM, but do not replace it. They also allow asset returns to be explained by factors other than the market index, and thus provide more specific information on risk analysis and the evaluation of manager performance.

In practice, analysts use models with "common factors," which affect all assets to a greater or lesser extent, and "sector or regional factors," which affect only some securities within a portfolio. Identification and prediction of truly pervasive factors is an extremely difficult task. Hence, the goal should be focused on permanent and important sources of asset and portfolio risk and return, not the transitory and unimportant phenomena that occur in any given period (Sharpe, 1985).

Steuer, Qi and Hirschberger (2007) focus on investors whose purpose is to build a suitable portfolio taking additional concerns into account. Such investors would have additional stochastic and deterministic objectives that might include dividends, number of securities in a portfolio, liquidity, social responsibility, and so forth. They develop a multiple criteria portfolio selection formulation.

Goal Programming (GP) is a pragmatic tool for analysing portfolio selection problems and reaching reasonable solutions in terms of the inclusion of the decision maker's preferences for risk and return factors (Jones and Tamiz, 2010). There are a vast number of other factors, here called extended factors, which can be considered. These extended factors include regional preferences and macroeconomic factors, as well as others. The use of one set of factors or another depends on the investor's attitudes and aspirations.

This chapter, therefore, investigates the incorporation of extended factors into various Goal Programming models for mutual funds portfolio selection and analysis.

7.2 Extended Factors Choice for Mutual Funds Portfolio Selection

7.2.1 Factors Specific to Mutual Funds

Carhart (1997) shows that mutual fund age is not related to its performance, in contrast to a later study by Gallagher (2002) who finds mutual fund performance to be influenced by mutual fund age.

Das et al. (2002) find mutual fund performance to be positively related to the total risk (as measured by the standard deviation).

The notion of risk has found practical application within the science of Risk Management and Risk Control. Deciding which types of risk to mitigate is the first dilemma of a decision maker and demands considerable attention. Focusing on one particular risk category may lead to a hedged portfolio for a particular source of risk but may result in exposure to other sources of risk.

According to the Sharpe (1966) model, the rate of return on any security is the result of two factors; a systematic component which is market related, and factors which are unique to a given security. In any application, however, concern should be not only with the alpha and beta, but with the level of uncertainty about the estimates as well.

Hu and Kercheval (2007) emphasise that portfolio optimisation requires balancing risk and return; one therefore needs to employ some precise concept of risk. The construction of an efficient frontier depends on two inputs: a choice of risk measure, such as standard deviation, value at risk, or expected shortfall; and a probability distribution used to model returns.

This chapter uses the standard deviation as a measure of risk, due to its ease of use and the availability of the underlying data. However, for similar experiments using more sophisticated risk measurements, the reader is referred to a research article by Tamiz, Azmi and Jones (2013). Many authors provide analysis of risk measures that go beyond standard deviation, such as Artzner et al. (1999), Balbas, Balbas and Mayoral (2009) and Rockafellar, Uryasev and Zabarankin (2006). Other relevant literature includes the following:

- Mansini, Ogryczak and Speranza (2007) study linear programs concerning solvable portfolio optimisation models based on extensions of the Conditional Value at Risk (CVaR) measure. The models use multiple CVaR measures, thus allowing for more detailed risk-aversion modelling.
- Pflug (2006) researches measures of risk in two categories: risk capital measures (which serve to determine the necessary amount of risk capital in order to avoid damage if the outcomes of an economic activity are uncertain, and their negative values may be interpreted as: acceptability measures, safety measures, and pure risk measures) and risk deviation measures (which are natural generalisations of the standard deviation).
- Rockafellar, Uryasev and Zabarankin (2006) systematically study general deviation measures for their potential applications to risk measurement in areas such as portfolio optimisation and engineering.
- Ogryczak and Ruszczynski (2002) analyse mean-risk models using quantiles and tail characteristics of the distribution. In particular, they emphasise value at risk (VAR) as a widely used quantile risk measure, which is defined as the maximum loss at a specified confidence level.
- Artzner et al. (1999) develop a coherent measure of risk in which they study both market risks and nonmarket risks, and discuss methods of measurement of these risks.
- Balbas, Balbas and Balbas (2009) discuss the portfolio choice problem and the classical APT and CAPM models when risk levels are given by risk measures beyond the variance.

- Balbas, Balbas and Mayoral (2009) emphasise that modern risk analysis must face two major drawbacks affecting most of the available securities and many investment strategies; namely: asymmetric returns and fat tails.

Although this chapter uses only three factors specific to mutual funds—namely fund age, total risk and return—there are other factors that could be investigated in further studies. For example, Volkman and Wohar (1995) and Gallagher (2002) claim the existence of positive relations between mutual fund performance and the fund's objective (income, growth or mixed). However, Peterson et al. (2001) find a negative relation between fund performance and fund's systematic risk. Other studies (e.g., Carhart, 1997) found no relation between fund performance and other fund factors such as size.

7.2.2 Factors for Macroeconomics

A basic premise of economics is that all economic decisions are made in the face of trade-offs, due to the scarcity of resources.

Investors need to know about an economy's market size, prices and productivity. The globalisation of markets for goods, services, finance, labour and ideas reinforces the interdependence of economies and the need to measure them on a common scale.

Converting Gross Domestic Product (GDP) and its components to a common currency using Purchasing Power Parity (PPP) leads to major revisions in the size and structure of world economies. PPP refers to the number of currency units required to purchase an amount of goods and services equivalent to what can be bought with one unit of currency of the base country, i.e., the U.S. dollar (a commonly used base currency). Unlike market exchange rates, PPPs adjust for differences in price levels between countries or economies and enable more robust cross-country comparisons (IMF, 2007).

Viewed through PPPs, low income economies produced 7% of global GDP in 2006, compared with 3% at market exchange rates. Middle income economies produced 33%, compared with 19% at market exchange rates. And high income economies produced 60% of world GDP at PPPs, compared with 78% at market exchange rates (IMF, 2006).

The global economy grew by 5% in 2006, with strong growth being maintained in emerging and developing countries, while growth in advanced economies slowed down. In the advanced economies, inflationary pressures eased, reflecting slowing demand; whereas in emerging economies, inflation rose in 2006 on account of strong domestic and external demand as well as higher food and energy prices. The current account balance was in deficit for the advanced economies, while that of emerging economies was positive (IMF, 2006; 2007).

7.2.3 Factor for Regional or Country Preferences

The economic indicators vary between countries, as does the viability of investment in certain countries.

Previous studies (for instance, Lehmann and Modest, 1987; Otten and Schweitzer, 2002) on the evaluation of the mutual fund's performance and portfolio selection problems in developed economies have provided varied results. In addition, there are some factors (such as the volatility of markets, the size of government involvement and the extent of regulations) which distinguish mutual funds in emerging markets from their counterparts in more established markets.

Therefore, the regional or country preferences influence the overall performance of a portfolio as some countries provide good investment opportunities and sustainable returns compared to others.

7.3 Experimental Data and Models Data

This chapter explores the portfolio selection problem at an international level, where the selection involves twenty mutual funds from ten different countries representing seven regions across the world. Such a selection usually involves many factors influencing the investment decision. Therefore, this chapter tries to represent more realistic cases for portfolio selection, exploring seven factors that belong to mutual fund attributes, macroeconomics and regional preferences.

The experiments use a constructing period of 84 weeks (April 2006 to December 2007) and 1,680 observations, and a testing period of 16 weeks (January 2008 to April 2008) and 320 observations. All the factors' data are as of December 2007.

The seven factors are shown in the following table for the twenty mutual funds across the globe, in columns headed RE, RI, AG, GD, CA, IN and RG respectively. The first column in the table shows the seven regions, the second column shows the ten countries from where the mutual funds are selected, and the third gives each mutual fund's name (these are the names' abbreviations that are shown in table A-4 with their long form, appendix D).

Table 7.1: Data of the 7 factors for 20 mutual funds used in GP's extended factors models

Region	Country	MF	Extended Factors						
			Mutual Funds Specific Factors			**Macroeconomic Factors**			**Regional Preferences**
			RE Average Return (%)	**RI** Total Risk (SD)	**AG** Fund Age (years)	**GD** GDP-PPP (%world's total)	**CA** Current Account (%GDP)	**IN** Annual Inflation (%)	**RG** Regional Preferences (10-70 Scores)
Middle East & North Africa - MENA	Egypt	E-E	0.88	0.099	13	0.53	0.8	4.2	10
		E-B	0.21	0.015	15	0.53	0.8	4.2	10
	KSA	K-C	-0.11	0.060	14	0.60	27.4	2.2	10
		K-S	-0.27	0.061	2	0.60	27.4	2.2	10
Asia Pacific	Japan	J-S	-0.19	0.021	7	6.30	3.9	0.3	50
		J-B	-0.52	0.026	21	6.30	3.9	0.3	50
	China	C-A	2.47	0.040	3	15.08	9.4	1.5	50
		C-I	2.11	0.037	6	15.08	9.4	1.5	50
Central Asia	India	I-R	0.94	0.039	12	6.28	-1.1	6.1	40
		I-B	1.03	0.042	5	6.28	-1.1	6.1	40
Western Europe	UK	U-A	0.38	0.027	6	3.20	-3.2	2.3	60
		U-S	0.23	0.025	37	3.20	-3.2	2.3	60
	Italy	T-I	0.32	0.021	16	2.70	-2.4	2.2	60
		T-F	0.30	0.020	12	2.70	-2.4	2.2	60
Eastern Europe	Russia	R-S	3.18	0.335	2	2.61	9.7	9.7	30
		R-U	0.75	0.031	18	2.61	9.7	9.7	30
North America	USA	S-B	0.22	0.016	31	19.66	-6.2	3.2	70
		S-A	0.17	0.018	14	19.66	-6.2	3.2	70
Latin America	Brazil	B-R	0.84	0.044	8	2.57	1.2	4.2	20
		B-F	1.00	0.046	2	2.57	1.2	4.2	20

Models

The decision maker's preferences can be incorporated into the GP models by the penalisation and weights assigned to the unwanted deviational variables, the target values set for each objective and the GP variants used.

Different deviational variable weights, sets of target values, and GP variants are explored in the following experiments and discussions of their relevance to the decision maker's preferences are given.

For the experiments reported in this chapter, the following strategy for the objective functions is adopted.

The "desired" level of achievement for each objective function and the penalisation of the respective deviational variables are:

- Return (RE) more than the target value (more is better; penalise negative deviational variable).
- Risk (RI) less than the target value (less is better; penalise positive deviational variable).
- Mutual Fund Age (AG) the same as the target value (exact achievement required; penalise both deviational variables).
- GDP in PPP (GD) more than the target value (more is better; penalise negative deviational variable).
- Current account (CA) the same as the target value (exact achievement required; penalise both deviational variables).
- Inflation (IN) less than the target value (less is better; penalise positive deviational variable).
- Regional Preferences Score (RG) the same as the target value (exact achievement required; penalise both deviational variables).

The objective functions in the GP models used in this chapter have target values which are strictly positive and measured in different units of measurement. Hence the GP models are ideally suited for the deployment of percentage normalisation (Tamiz and Jones, 1997), whereby the unwanted deviational variables' weight for each objective in the achievement function is divided by its respective target value.

7.3.1 The Weighted Goal Programming Model

$$Min\left(\frac{\alpha_{RE}}{b_{RE}}n_{RE}+\frac{\alpha_{RI}}{b_{RI}}n_{RI}+\frac{\alpha_{AG}}{b_{AG}}n_{AG}+\frac{\alpha_{GD}}{b_{GD}}n_{GD}+\frac{\alpha_{CA}}{b_{CA}}n_{CA}+\frac{\alpha_{IN}}{b_{IN}}n_{IN}+\frac{\alpha_{RG}}{b_{RG}}n_{RG}+\frac{\beta_{RE}}{b_{RE}}p_{RE}+\frac{\beta_{RI}}{b_{RI}}p_{RI}+\frac{\beta_{AG}}{b_{AG}}p_{AG}+\frac{\beta_{GD}}{b_{GD}}p_{GD}+\frac{\beta_{CA}}{b_{CA}}p_{CA}+\frac{\beta_{IN}}{b_{IN}}p_{IN}+\frac{\beta_{RG}}{b_{RG}}p_{RG}\right)$$

Subject to:

$$\sum_{j=1}^{20} RE_j X_j + n_{RE} - p_{RE} = b_{RE}$$
$$\sum_{j=1}^{20} RI_j X_j + n_{RI} - p_{RI} = b_{RI}$$
$$\sum_{j=1}^{20} AG_j X_j + n_{AG} - p_{AG} = b_{AG}$$
$$\sum_{j=1}^{20} GD_j X_j + n_{GD} - p_{GD} = b_{GD}$$
$$\sum_{j=1}^{20} CA_j X_j + n_{CA} - p_{CA} = b_{CA}$$
$$\sum_{j=1}^{20} IN_j X_j + n_{IN} - p_{IN} = b_{IN}$$
$$\sum_{j=1}^{20} RG_j X_j + n_{RG} - p_{RG} = b_{RG}$$
$$\sum_{j=1}^{20} X_j = 1$$
$$X_j \geq 0 \quad j = 1, \ldots, 20$$
$$All\ negative\ and\ positive\ deviations \geq 0$$

The experiments are carried out according to the following sequence of models:

First: The Baseline Model

The baseline model has weights of 1 (i.e., there are no preferred weights) for each of the seven factors (objectives). The target values are set reasonably close to the world's averages for each factor as shown in the following table.

Table 7.2: The baseline WGP model parameter

Extended Factors	Deviational Variables Weights	Target Values (b_i)	World Averages
RE: Return (%)	$\alpha_{RE} = 1$, $\beta_{RE} = 0$	b_{RE}= 0.015	0.010
RI: Risk (measured by the standard deviation)	$\alpha_{RI} = 0$, $\beta_{RI} = 1$	b_{RI}= 0.030	0.040
AG: MF Age (years)	$\alpha_{AG} = 1$, $\beta_{AG} = 1$	b_{AG}= 13.0	12.0
GD: GDP/PPP (% of world's total)	$\alpha_{GD} = 1$, $\beta_{GD} = 0$	b_{GD}= 0.07	0.06
CA: Current Account balance (% of the GDP)	$\alpha_{CA} = 1$, $\beta_{CA} = 1$	b_{CA}= 0.05	0.04
IN: Inflation (% annual change)	$\alpha_{IN} = 0$, $\beta_{IN} = 1$	b_{IN}= 0.03	0.04
RG: Regional Preferences (scored from 10 to 70 points)	$\alpha_{RG} = 1$, $\beta_{RG} = 1$	b_{RG}= 35.0	35.0

Second: The WGP models with different weights

The WGP models of different deviational variable weights are shown in the following table.

Table 7.3: The WGP models with different weightings for the unwanted deviational variables

Extended Factors	Baseline Deviational Variable Weights	W1	W2	W3
RE	$\alpha_{RE} = 1$, $\beta_{RE} = 0$	$\alpha_{RE} = 5$, $\beta_{RE} = 0$	$\alpha_{RE} = 1$, $\beta_{RE} = 0$	$\alpha_{RE} = 1$, $\beta_{RE} = 0$
RI	$\alpha_{RI} = 0$, $\beta_{RI} = 1$	$\alpha_{RI} = 0$, $\beta_{RI} = 10$	$\alpha_{RI} = 0$, $\beta_{RI} = 1$	$\alpha_{RI} = 0$, $\beta_{RI} = 5$
AG	$\alpha_{AG} = 1$, $\beta_{AG} = 1$	$\alpha_{AG} = 2$, $\beta_{AG} = 2$	$\alpha_{AG} = 1$, $\beta_{AG} = 1$	$\alpha_{AG} = 1$, $\beta_{AG} = 1$
GD	$\alpha_{GD} = 1$, $\beta_{GD} = 0$	$\alpha_{GD} = 1$, $\beta_{GD} = 0$	$\alpha_{GD} = 10$, $\beta_{GD} = 0$	$\alpha_{GD} = 1$, $\beta_{GD} = 0$
CA	$\alpha_{CA} = 1$, $\beta_{CA} = 1$	$\alpha_{CA} = 1$, $\beta_{CA} = 1$	$\alpha_{CA} = 5$, $\beta_{CA} = 5$	$\alpha_{CA} = 1$, $\beta_{CA} = 1$
IN	$\alpha_{IN} = 0$, $\beta_{IN} = 1$	$\alpha_{IN} = 0$, $\beta_{IN} = 1$	$\alpha_{IN} = 0$, $\beta_{IN} = 2$	$\alpha_{IN} = 0$, $\beta_{IN} = 1$
RG	$\alpha_{RG} = 1$, $\beta_{RG} = 1$	$\alpha_{RG} = 1$, $\beta_{RG} = 1$	$\alpha_{RG} = 1$, $\beta_{RG} = 1$	$\alpha_{RG} = 5$, $\beta_{RG} = 5$

The highlighted part of each column represents the weight differences from the baseline model. W1, W2 and W3 represent possible preferences in investment decision making based on the seven available factors. W1 gives high weights for return, risk and fund age (mutual funds specific factors), while W2 gives the high weights for the macroeconomic factors (the share of the country in the world GDP in PPP, current account balance as a percent of GDP and inflation rate). W3 gives high weighting for both risk and regional preferences.

Third: The WGP models with different target values

The WGP models of different target values are shown in the following table.

Table 7.4: The WGP models with changed target values for some factors

Factors' Target Values	Baseline Target Values	W4	W5	W6	W7
b_{RE}=	0.015	0.015	0.015	0.015	0.015
b_{RI}=	0.03	0.010	0.030	0.030	0.030
b_{AG}=	13.0	13.0	13.0	13.0	13.0
b_{GD}=	0.07	0.07	0.20	0.07	0.07
b_{CA}=	0.05	0.05	0.05	0.05	0.05
b_{IN}=	0.03	0.03	0.03	0.03	0.03
b_{RG}=	35	35	35	70	10

The highlighted part of each column represents the target value differences from the baseline model. W4, W5, W6 and W7 represent another type of preferences in investment decision making.

An investor might decide that the world average for mutual funds risk is not good enough and hence seek to reach a risk which is significantly lower than the world average, say 0.01 instead of 0.03, which is the case for W4.

In W5 the target value for a country's share in the world GDP in PPP is changed from 0.07 to 0.20. This might be the case for an investor who decides on investing in a country (through its mutual funds) based on its share in the world GDP and seeks the highest share across the globe.

Assuming that an investor is interested in a specific region according to his/her own analysis and risk tolerance, models W6 and W7 are set up to represent two different regional preferences relative to the baseline case of 35. The aim for W6 is to invest in the North America region, which has a score of 70, while the aim in W7 is to invest in the Middle East and North Africa region, which has the score of 10.

7.3.2 The Lexicographic Goal Programming Model

The achievement function of the Lexicographic Goal Programming (LGP) model for this section consists of two priority levels which are lexicographically minimised subject to the same objectives of the WGP model.

The weights for the unwanted deviational variables in LGP models are kept the same as in WGP models for the purpose of comparing the performance of the resulting portfolios. The unwanted deviational variables are further grouped in two priority levels, indicating that achieving the objectives in the first priority level is infinitely more important than achieving the objectives in the second priority level.

The LGP experiments are carried out according to the following sequence of models:

First: The Baseline Model

Table 7.5: The baseline LGP model

Extended Factors	Priority Levels of the Baseline LGP Model		Baseline Target Values
	Priority Level 1 [h_1]	Priority Level 2 [h_2]	
RE	$\alpha_{RE} = 1$, $\beta_{RE} = 0$		b_{RE}= 0.015
RI	$\alpha_{RI} = 0$, $\beta_{RI} = 1$		b_{RI}= 0.030
AG	$\alpha_{AG} = 1$, $\beta_{AG} = 1$		b_{AG}= 13.0
GD		$\alpha_{GD} = 1$, $\beta_{GD} = 0$	b_{GD}= 0.07
CA		$\alpha_{CA} = 1$, $\beta_{CA} = 1$	b_{CA}= 0.05
IN		$\alpha_{IN} = 0$, $\beta_{IN} = 1$	b_{IN}= 0.03
RG		$\alpha_{RG} = 1$, $\beta_{RG} = 1$	b_{RG}= 35.0

The highlighted part of each column represents the priority levels with the weights on their deviational variables.

The LGP for the baseline model is as follows:

$$Lex\ Min\ \boldsymbol{a} = h_1\left[\frac{1}{0.015}n_{RE}, \frac{1}{0.03}p_{RI}, \frac{1}{13}(n_{AG} + p_{AG})\right],$$
$$h_2\left[\frac{1}{0.07}n_{GD}, \frac{1}{0.05}(n_{CA} + p_{CA}), \frac{1}{0.03}p_{IN}, \frac{1}{35}(n_{RG} + p_{RG})\right]$$

Subject to:

$$\sum_{j=1}^{20} RE_j X_j + n_{RE} - p_{RE} = 0.015$$

$$\sum_{j=1}^{20} RI_j X_j + n_{RI} - p_{RI} = 0.03$$

$$\sum_{j=1}^{20} AG_j X_j + n_{AG} - p_{AG} = 13$$

$$\sum_{j=1}^{20} GD_j X_j + n_{GD} - p_{GD} = 0.07$$

$$\sum_{j=1}^{20} CA_j X_j + n_{CA} - p_{CA} = 0.05$$

$$\sum_{j=1}^{20} IN_j X_j + n_{IN} - p_{IN} = 0.03$$

$$\sum_{j=1}^{20} RG_j X_j + n_{RG} - p_{RG} = 35$$

$$\sum_{j=1}^{20} X_j = 1$$

$$X_j \geq 0 \qquad j = 1, \ldots, 20$$

$$All\ negative\ and\ positive\ deviations \geq 0$$

Second: The LGP Models with Different Weights and Priority Levels

Three experiments are conducted with different weightings for the unwanted deviational variables and different priority levels as shown in the following table.

Table 7.6: The LGP models with different weightings for the unwanted deviational variables

Extended Factors	Priority Levels for L1		Priority Levels for L2		Priority Levels for L3	
	Priority Level 1 [h_1]	Priority Level 2 [h_2]	Priority Level 1 [h_1]	Priority Level 2 [h_2]	Priority Level 1 [h_1]	Priority Level 2 [h_2]
RE	$\alpha_{RE} = 5$, $\beta_{RE} = 0$			$\alpha_{RE} = 1$, $\beta_{RE} = 0$		$\alpha_{RE} = 1$, $\beta_{RE} = 0$
RI	$\alpha_{RI} = 0$, $\beta_{RI} = 10$			$\alpha_{RI} = 0$, $\beta_{RI} = 1$	$\alpha_{RI} = 0$, $\beta_{RI} = 5$	
AG	$\alpha_{AG} = 2$, $\beta_{AG} = 2$			$\alpha_{AG} = 1$, $\beta_{AG} = 1$		$\alpha_{AG} = 1$, $\beta_{AG} = 1$
GD		$\alpha_{GD} = 1$, $\beta_{GD} = 0$	$\alpha_{GD} = 10$, $\beta_{GD} = 0$			$\alpha_{GD} = 1$, $\beta_{GD} = 0$
CA		$\alpha_{CA} = 1$, $\beta_{CA} = 1$	$\alpha_{CA} = 5$, $\beta_{CA} = 5$			$\alpha_{CA} = 1$, $\beta_{CA} = 1$
IN		$\alpha_{IN} = 0$, $\beta_{IN} = 1$	$\alpha_{IN} = 0$, $\beta_{IN} = 2$			$\alpha_{IN} = 0$, $\beta_{IN} = 1$
RG		$\alpha_{RG} = 1$, $\beta_{RG} = 1$	$\alpha_{RG} = 1$, $\beta_{RG} = 1$		$\alpha_{RG} = 5$, $\beta_{RG} = 5$	

The priority levels and the weightings of the unwanted deviational variables for LGP models L1, L2 and L3 are shown in table 7.6. These priority levels and weightings are set out to reflect the decision maker preferences. For instance, L1 gives higher weights than the baseline model for return, risk and fund age (mutual funds specific factors) within priority level 1.

Third: The LGP Models with Different Target Values

The LGP models of different factors' target values are shown in the following table.

Table 7.7: The LGP models of changed target values for some factors

Extended Factors	Baseline LGP Model Priority Level 1 $[h_1(n,p)]$	Baseline LGP Model Priority Level 2 $[h_2(n,p)]$	b_i	**L4**	**L5**	**L6**	**L7**
RE	$\alpha_{RE}=1$, $\beta_{RE}=0$		b_{RE}= 0.015	b_{RE}= 0.015	b_{RE}= 0.015	b_{RE}= 0.015	b_{RE}= 0.015
RI	$\alpha_{RI}=0$, $\beta_{RI}=1$		b_{RI}= 0.03	b_{RI}= 0.010	b_{RI}= 0.030	b_{RI}= 0.030	b_{RI}= 0.030
AG	$\alpha_{AG}=1$, $\beta_{AG}=1$		b_{AG}= 13.0	b_{AG}= 13.0	b_{AG}= 13.0	b_{AG}= 13.0	b_{AG}= 13.0
GD		$\alpha_{GD}=1$, $\beta_{GD}=0$	b_{GD}= 0.07	b_{GD}= 0.07	b_{GD}= 0.20	b_{GD}= 0.07	b_{GD}= 0.07
CA		$\alpha_{CA}=1$, $\beta_{CA}=1$	b_{CA}= 0.05	b_{CA}= 0.05	b_{CA}= 0.05	b_{CA}= 0.05	b_{CA}= 0.05
IN		$\alpha_{IN}=0$, $\beta_{IN}=1$	b_{IN}= 0.03	b_{IN}= 0.03	b_{IN}= 0.03	b_{IN}= 0.03	b_{IN}= 0.03
RG		$\alpha_{RG}=1$, $\beta_{RG}=1$	b_{RG}= 35.0	b_{RG}= 35.0	b_{RG}= 35.0	b_{RG}= 70.0	b_{RG}= 10.0

L4, L5, L6 and L7 represent the cases where an investor might be interested in higher or lower target values for some of the factors within the priority level set in the baseline model. L4 and L5 change the target value for RI and GD, while L6 and L7 represent two different regional preferences relative to the baseline case.

7.3.3 The MinMax Goal Programming Model

Minimise λ

Subject to:

$$\frac{\alpha_{RE}}{b_{RE}} n_{RE} + \frac{\beta_{RE}}{b_{RE}} p_{RE} - \lambda \leq 0$$

$$\frac{\alpha_{RI}}{b_{RI}} n_{RI} + \frac{\beta_{RI}}{b_{RI}} p_{RI} - \lambda \leq 0$$

$$\frac{\alpha_{AG}}{b_{AG}} n_{AG} + \frac{\beta_{AG}}{b_{AG}} p_{AG} - \lambda \leq 0$$

$$\frac{\alpha_{GD}}{b_{GD}} n_{GD} + \frac{\beta_{GD}}{b_{GD}} p_{GD} - \lambda \leq 0$$

$$\frac{\alpha_{CA}}{b_{CA}} n_{CA} + \frac{\beta_{CA}}{b_{CA}} p_{CA} - \lambda \leq 0$$
$$\frac{\alpha_{IN}}{b_{IN}} n_{IN} + \frac{\beta_{IN}}{b_{IN}} p_{IN} - \lambda \leq 0$$
$$\frac{\alpha_{RG}}{b_{RG}} n_{RG} + \frac{\beta_{RG}}{b_{RG}} p_{RG} - \lambda \leq 0$$

$$\sum_{j=1}^{20} RE_j X_j + n_{RE} - p_{RE} = b_{RE}$$

$$\sum_{j=1}^{20} RI_j X_j + n_{RI} - p_{RI} = b_{RI}$$

$$\sum_{j=1}^{20} AG_j X_j + n_{AG} - p_{AG} = b_{AG}$$

$$\sum_{j=1}^{20} GD_j X_j + n_{GD} - p_{GD} = b_{GD}$$

$$\sum_{j=1}^{20} CA_j X_j + n_{CA} - p_{CA} = b_{CA}$$

$$\sum_{j=1}^{20} IN_j X_j + n_{IN} - p_{IN} = b_{IN}$$

$$\sum_{j=1}^{20} RG_j X_j + n_{RG} - p_{RG} = b_{RG}$$

$$\sum_{j=1}^{20} X_j = 1$$

$$X_j \geq 0 \quad j = 1, \dots, 20$$

$$All\ negative\ and\ positive\ deviations \geq 0$$

The MinMax GP experiments are carried out according to the following table:

Table 7.8: The MinMax GP experimental models

Extended Factors	First: Baseline MinMax GP Model		Second: MinMax GP models after changing some deviational variable weights			Third: MinMax GP models after changing some factors' target values				
	Deviational variable Weights	b_i	Deviational Variable Weights			b_i	Target Values			
			M1	M2	M3		M4	M5	M6	M7
RE	$\alpha_{RE}=1$, $\beta_{RE}=0$	$b_{RE}=$ 0.015	$\alpha_{RE}=5$, $\beta_{RE}=0$	$\alpha_{RE}=1$, $\beta_{RE}=0$	$\alpha_{RE}=1$, $\beta_{RE}=0$	$b_{RE}=$	0.015	0.015	0.015	0.015
RI	$\alpha_{RI}=0$, $\beta_{RI}=1$	$b_{RI}=$ 0.03	$\alpha_{RI}=0$, $\beta_{RI}=10$	$\alpha_{RI}=0$, $\beta_{RI}=1$	$\alpha_{RI}=0$, $\beta_{RI}=5$	$b_{RI}=$	0.010	0.030	0.030	0.030
AG	$\alpha_{AG}=1$, $\beta_{AG}=1$	$b_{AG}=$ 13.0	$\alpha_{AG}=2$, $\beta_{AG}=2$	$\alpha_{AG}=1$, $\beta_{AG}=1$	$\alpha_{AG}=1$, $\beta_{AG}=1$	$b_{AG}=$	13.0	13.0	13.0	13.0
GD	$\alpha_{GD}=1$, $\beta_{GD}=0$	$b_{GD}=$ 0.07	$\alpha_{GD}=1$, $\beta_{GD}=0$	$\alpha_{GD}=10$, $\beta_{GD}=0$	$\alpha_{GD}=1$, $\beta_{GD}=0$	$b_{GD}=$	0.07	0.20	0.07	0.07
CA	$\alpha_{CA}=1$, $\beta_{CA}=1$	$b_{CA}=$ 0.05	$\alpha_{CA}=1$, $\beta_{CA}=1$	$\alpha_{CA}=5$, $\beta_{CA}=5$	$\alpha_{CA}=1$, $\beta_{CA}=1$	$b_{CA}=$	0.05	0.05	0.05	0.05
IN	$\alpha_{IN}=0$, $\beta_{IN}=1$	$b_{IN}=$ 0.03	$\alpha_{IN}=0$, $\beta_{IN}=1$	$\alpha_{IN}=0$, $\beta_{IN}=2$	$\alpha_{IN}=0$, $\beta_{IN}=1$	$b_{IN}=$	0.03	0.03	0.03	0.03
RG	$\alpha_{RG}=1$, $\beta_{RG}=1$	$b_{RG}=$ 35.0	$\alpha_{RG}=1$, $\beta_{RG}=1$	$\alpha_{RG}=1$, $\beta_{RG}=1$	$\alpha_{RG}=5$, $\beta_{RG}=5$	$b_{RG}=$	35	35	70	10

Table 7.8 shows the different MinMax GP models, where for comparison purposes the weights on unwanted deviational variables in M1, M2 and M3 are the same as in W1, W2 and W3, while the target values in M4, M5, M6 and M7 are the same as the target values in W4, W5, W6 and W7, respectively.

7.4 The Resulting Portfolios and their Comparisons

The various GP models utilised in this chapter have selected interesting portfolios in terms of the factors considered. In order to compare and analyse the constructed portfolios, the following basic investment criteria are investigated for each of the selected portfolio:

- Return: the average return is calculated for the portfolio.
- Risk: the total risk measured by the standard deviation.
- Cost: there is not enough data to calculate the actual costs involved when deciding to invest in a certain mutual fund located in a

country. However, generally, the more mutual funds included in a portfolio, the higher the cost both for setting up and rebalancing. This is even more compelling for investments in different countries and regions (due to differences in financial, technological, political, economic, exchange rates, social and legal conditions across countries), as is the case with this chapter's experiments.

Furthermore, the models are analysed in terms of their ability to achieve the targets for all the factors considered.

7.4.1 Results of WGP Models

The following table shows the results for the WGP-constructed portfolios, namely: return, risk, selected mutual funds (name, country and proportions) as well as percentage of achievement for each target value of the seven factors.

Table 7.9 shows the results of the eight WGP models examined in this chapter. The WGP baseline model selects a portfolio of six mutual funds from five countries, with a return of -0.003 and risk of 0.03. The model has 100% achievement for five of the factors involved, while the percentage achievements of the remaining factors are 81% for RE and 104% for GD.

W1 selects four mutual funds from four countries and its portfolio has a return and risk of -0.003 and 0.037 respectively. W1 produces the same return compared to the baseline model but with higher risk. The percentage achievements for the factors are 81%, 83% for AG and IN respectively, RE, RI and CA have 100% achievement, and the percentage achievements of the remaining factors are 149% for the GD and 114% for the RG. Therefore, the baseline model appears to produce a better portfolio than W1. Although higher weights were assigned to return and risk in W1, the model's portfolio was not able to attain the same achievement rates for most of the factors and did not generate higher return or lower risk.

Table 7.9: The results of the WGP models

WGP Models		Return	Risk	Selected Mutual Funds		% of Achievement for each target value for the 7 factors		
				MFs (Country)	Proportions (%)	b_i	Achieved	%
First: The baseline model		**-0.003**	**0.030**	E-E (Egypt) E-B (Egypt) K-C (KSA) C-A (China) U-S (UK) R-U (Russia) Total: 6 MFs	1.13 35.09 2.23 43.18 13.51 4.86	b_{RE}=0.015 b_{RI}=0.030 b_{AG}=13.0 b_{GD}=0.07 b_{CA}=0.05 b_{IN}=0.03 b_{RG}=35.0	**0.012** **0.030** **13.0** **0.07** **0.05** **0.03** **35.0**	**81** **100** **100** **104** **100** **100** **100**
Second: The models changing deviational variable weights	W1	**-0.003**	**0.037**	E-B (Egypt) C-A (China) S-B (USA) U-S (UK) Total: 4 MFs	30.55 57.16 7.46 4.84	b_{RE}=0.015 b_{RI}=0.030 b_{AG}=13.0 b_{GD}=0.07 b_{CA}=0.05 b_{IN}=0.03 b_{RG}=35.0	**0.015** **0.030** **10.5** **0.10** **0.05** **0.02** **39.8**	**100** **100** **81** **149** **100** **83** **114**
	W2	**-0.003**	**0.030**	E-E (Egypt) E-B (Egypt) K-C (KSA) C-A (China) U-S (UK) R-U (Russia) Total: 6 MFs	1.13 35.09 2.23 43.18 13.51 4.86	b_{RE}=0.015 b_{RI}=0.030 b_{AG}=13.0 b_{GD}=0.07 b_{CA}=0.05 b_{IN}=0.03 b_{RG}=35.0	**0.012** **0.030** **13.0** **0.07** **0.05** **0.03** **35.0**	**81** **100** **100** **104** **100** **100** **100**
	W3	**-0.003**	**0.030**	E-E (Egypt) E-B (Egypt) K-C (KSA) C-A (China) U-S (UK) R-U (Russia) Total: 6 MFs	1.13 35.09 2.23 43.18 13.51 4.86	b_{RE}=0.015 b_{RI}=0.030 b_{AG}=13.0 b_{GD}=0.07 b_{CA}=0.05 b_{IN}=0.03 b_{RG}=35.0	**0.012** **0.030** **13.0** **0.07** **0.05** **0.03** **35.0**	**81** **100** **100** **104** **100** **100** **100**
Third: The models changing some factors' target values	W4	**-0.004**	**0.025**	E-B (Egypt) K-C (KSA) C-I (China) U-S (UK) R-U (Russia) Total: 5 MFs	37.07 0.55 46.84 10.53 5.01	b_{RE}=0.015 **b_{RI}=0.010** b_{AG}=13.0 b_{GD}=0.07 b_{CA}=0.05 b_{IN}=0.03 b_{RG}=35.0	**0.011** **0.028** **13.0** **0.08** **0.05** **0.03** **35.0**	**75** **275** **100** **110** **100** **100** **100**
	W5	**-0.005**	**0.028**	E-B (Egypt) C-A (China) C-I (China) R-U (Russia) S-B (USA) Total: 5 MFs	11.73 20.11 36.35 9.88 21.93	b_{RE}=0.015 b_{RI}=0.030 b_{AG}=13.0 **b_{GD}=0.20** b_{CA}=0.05 b_{IN}=0.03 b_{RG}=35.0	**0.014** **0.030** **13.0** **0.13** **0.05** **0.03** **47.7**	**94** **100** **100** **66** **100** **100** **136**
	W6	**-0.007**	**0.030**	J-S (Japan) C-I (China) R-U (Russia) S-B (USA) Total: 4 MFs	2.13 67.21 3.15 27.51	b_{RE}=0.015 b_{RI}=0.030 b_{AG}=13.0 b_{GD}=0.07 b_{CA}=0.05 b_{IN}=0.03 **b_{RG}=70.0**	**0.015** **0.031** **13.0** **0.16** **0.05** **0.02** **54.9**	**100** **103** **100** **225** **100** **73** **78**
	W7	**0.001**	**0.024**	E-E (Egypt) E-B (Egypt) K-C (KSA) C-A (China) Total: 4 MFs	7.30 67.19 11.14 14.37	b_{RE}=0.015 b_{RI}=0.030 b_{AG}=13.0 b_{GD}=0.07 b_{CA}=0.05 b_{IN}=0.03 **b_{RG}=10.0**	**0.015** **0.030** **13.0** **0.03** **0.05** **0.04** **15.7**	**36** **100** **100** **38** **100** **120** **157**

W2 and W3 select exactly the same portfolios picked by the baseline model with similar achievement rates as well as risk and return levels. This result implies that even though W2 assigns higher weighting for macroeconomic factors and W3 assigns higher weighting for risk and regional preferences, both models could not improve the portfolio selection process in terms of risk, return and achievement levels for other factors. It could be implied that the macroeconomic factors were already taken care of in the baseline model (although with equal weights) and there was no room for further improvements. The same analogy applies to W3 (risk and region) where there was no possibility for further improvements and hence the model selects the same portfolio as that of the baseline model.

This result also means that the target values set for each of the seven factors are realistic and achievable to the extent that there was no room for further improvement. Other possibilities that an investor might be interested to explore are setting challenging target values to generate portfolios that could beat the world average, and such possibilities are explored with the W4, W5, W6 and W7 experiments.

W4 selects five mutual funds (from five countries) with an average return of -0.004 and risk level of 0.025, while W5 provides -0.005 return associated with 0.028 risk in a portfolio of five mutual funds. When compared to the baseline model, W4 generates a lower risk but with lower return as well. W5 has a lower return with slightly lower risk, compared to the baseline portfolio.

W6 selects four mutual funds with a return of -0.007 (less than the baseline portfolio return) and a risk of 0.030 (same risk as the baseline portfolio). The aim in W6 is to increase investing in the North America region but that preference seems to adversely impact the return of the selected portfolio.

W7, in contrast to W6, has a return of +0.001 and a risk of 0.024, which are both better than the baseline portfolio. W7's aim is to invest more in the Middle East and North Africa region. The resulting portfolio generates better return and risk levels, but this selection adversely affects the achievement levels for some factors. Specifically, W7 has 100% achievement for three of the factors involved, while the percentage achievements of the remaining factors are 36% for RE, 38% for GD, 120% for IN, and 157% for RG. W7 appears to be the only experiment from the WGP experiments that has a major underachievement in some factors. It appears that a specific preference to one region could mean sacrificing other factors. The decision maker should decide in such case about the importance and the priority of each factor in order to be able to sacrifice some factors if they are less important than others. In fact, an investor could decide that the achievement of some factors is infinitely more important than achieving the others. Such decisions are investigated using LGP models.

7.4.2 Results of LGP Models

The following table shows the results of LGP model experiments.

Table 7.10: The results of LGP models

LGP Models		Return	Risk	Selected Mutual Funds		% of achievement for each target value for the 7 factors		
				MFs (Country)	Proportions (%)	b_i	Achieved	%
First: The baseline model		-0.004	0.034	C-A (China) E-B (Egypt) U-S (UK) S-B (USA) Total: 4 MFs	57.09 14.89 3.29 24.73	b_{RE}=0.015 b_{RI}=0.030 b_{AG}=13.0 b_{GD}=0.07 b_{CA}=0.05 b_{IN}=0.03 b_{RG}=35.0	**0.015** **0.030** **13.0** **0.14** **0.04** **0.02** **49.3**	**100** **100** **100** **195** **77** **78** **141**
Second: The models changing deviational variable weights	**L1**	-0.004	0.034	C-A (China) E-B (Egypt) U-S (UK) S-B (USA) Total: 4 MFs	57.09 14.89 3.29 24.73	b_{RE}=0.015 b_{RI}=0.030 b_{AG}=13.0 b_{GD}=0.07 b_{CA}=0.05 b_{IN}=0.03 b_{RG}=35.0	**0.015** **0.030** **13.0** **0.14** **0.04** **0.02** **49.3**	**100** **100** **100** **195** **77** **78** **141**
	L2	-0.003	0.030	E-E (Egypt) E-B (Egypt) K-C (KSA) C-A (China) U-S (UK) R-U (Russia) Total: 6 MFs	1.13 35.09 2.23 43.18 13.51 4.86	b_{RE}=0.015 b_{RI}=0.030 b_{AG}=13.0 b_{GD}=0.07 b_{CA}=0.05 b_{IN}=0.03 b_{RG}=35.0	**0.012** **0.030** **13.0** **0.07** **0.05** **0.03** **35.0**	**81** **100** **100** **104** **100** **100** **100**
	L3	-0.003	0.030	E-E (Egypt) E-B (Egypt) K-C (KSA) C-A (China) U-S (UK) R-U (Russia) Total: 6 MFs	1.13 35.09 2.23 43.18 13.51 4.86	b_{RE}=0.015 b_{RI}=0.030 b_{AG}=13.0 b_{GD}=0.07 b_{CA}=0.05 b_{IN}=0.03 b_{RG}=35.0	**0.012** **0.030** **13.0** **0.07** **0.05** **0.03** **35.0**	**81** **100** **100** **104** **100** **100** **100**

Third: The models changing some factors' target values	**L4**	**0.004**	**0.023**	E-B (Egypt) Total: 1 MF	100	b_{RE}=0.015 **b_{RI}=0.010** b_{AG}=13.0 b_{GD}=0.07 b_{CA}=0.05 b_{IN}=0.03 b_{RG}=35.0	**0.002** **0.015** **14.8** **0.00** **0.00** **0.04** **10.0**	**14** **153** **114** **8** **16** **140** **29**
	L5	**-0.005**	**0.032**	E-B (Egypt) C-A (China) C-1 (China) S-B (USA) Total: 4 MFs	9.72 31.52 30.32 28.43	b_{RE}=0.015 b_{RI}=0.030 b_{AG}=13.0 **b_{GD}=0.20** b_{CA}=0.05 b_{IN}=0.03 b_{RG}=35.0	**0.015** **0.030** **13.0** **0.15** **0.04** **0.02** **51.8**	**100** **100** **100** **75** **83** **75** **148**
	L6	**-0.005**	**0.032**	E-B (Egypt) C-A (China) C-1 (China) S-B (USA) Total: 4 MFs	9.72 31.52 30.32 28.43	b_{RE}=0.015 b_{RI}=0.030 b_{AG}=13.0 b_{GD}=0.07 b_{CA}=0.05 b_{IN}=0.03 **b_{RG}=70.0**	**0.015** **0.030** **13.0** **0.15** **0.04** **0.02** **51.8**	**100** **100** **100** **214** **83** **75** **74**
	L7	**-0.004**	**0.034**	C-A (China) E-B (Egypt) U-S (UK) S-B (USA) Total: 4 MFs	57.09 14.89 3.29 24.73	b_{RE}=0.015 b_{RI}=0.030 b_{AG}=13.0 b_{GD}=0.07 b_{CA}=0.05 b_{IN}=0.03 **b_{RG}=10.0**	**0.015** **0.030** **13.0** **0.14** **0.04** **0.02** **49.3**	**100** **100** **100** **195** **77** **78** **493**

Table 7.10 shows the results of eight LGP models, where the baseline model generates -0.004 return and 0.034 risk through selecting four mutual funds from four countries. The baseline's percentage achievement is 100% for all of the three factors included in priority level 1.

L1 selects the same mutual funds as in the baseline portfolio, with the same risk and return. This result is expected since L1 has exactly the same priority levels as in the baseline, but with higher weights for the unwanted deviational variables in priority level 1.

L2 selects a portfolio of six mutual funds and achieves higher returns compared to the baseline portfolio with a lower risk of 0.030. Furthermore, it has higher levels of achievement for most of the factors. The percentage achievement is 100% for five factors, compared to three factors with 100% achievement in the baseline model. This is interesting since the baseline model gives priority level 1 to mutual funds specific factors, while L2 model gives priority level 1 and higher weights to macroeconomics.

L3 could not improve in terms of return and risk compared to L2, although the priority levels are different. However, L3 and L2 achieve higher returns and lower risk compared to the baseline model. Comparing the LGP baseline model, L1, L2 and L3 imply that giving the first priority to macroeconomic factors or risk and regional preferences produces better-performing portfolios.

L4 selects only one mutual fund with the highest return amongst all LGP portfolios and a lower risk compared to the baseline model, at the expense of a lower percentage of achievements for some factors, most notably GD (with an achievement percentage of 8%). It is interesting that the mutual fund selected in L4 has in fact the lowest risk amongst the 20 mutual funds.

L5 produces a portfolio of four mutual funds, generating lower returns and lower risk compared to the baseline portfolio. L6 produces the same portfolio as in L5, with the same percentage achievement for five of the factors.

L7 generates exactly the same return and risk levels as in baseline model with the same percentage achievements for six of the factors. The percentage achievement changes only for the factor whose target value is changed.

7.4.3 Results of MinMax GP Models

The following table illustrates the results of the MinMax GP experiments.

Table 7.11: The results of the MinMax GP models

MinMax GP Models		Return	Risk	Selected Mutual Funds		% of Achievement for each target value for the 7 factors		
				MFs (Country)	Proportions (%)	b_i	Achieved	%
First: The baseline model		**-0.003**	**0.033**	E-E (Egypt) E-B (Egypt) C-A (China) U-S (UK) R-U(Russia) Total: 5 MFs	2.47 27.20 49.38 12.00 8.14	b_{RE}=0.015 b_{RI}=0.030 b_{AC}=13.0 b_{GD}=0.07 b_{CA}=0.05 b_{IN}=0.03 b_{RC}=35.0	**0.014** **0.032** **12.1** **0.08** **0.05** **0.03** **37.5**	**93** **107** **93** **117** **107** **104** **107**
Second: The models changing deviational variable weights	M1	**-0.003**	**0.036**	E-B (Egypt) C-A (China) U-S (UK) S-B (USA) Total: 4 MFs	28.84 55.12 15.62 0.43	b_{RE}=0.015 b_{RI}=0.030 b_{AC}=13.0 b_{GD}=0.07 b_{CA}=0.05 b_{IN}=0.03 b_{RC}=35.0	**0.015** **0.030** **12.1** **0.09** **0.05** **0.02** **40.1**	**97** **101** **93** **129** **98** **80** **115**
	M2	**-0.003**	**0.033**	E-E (Egypt) E-B (Egypt) C-A (China) U-S (UK) R-U(Russia) Total: 5 MFs	2.85 28.80 50.11 12.86 5.37	b_{RE}=0.015 b_{RI}=0.030 b_{AC}=13.0 b_{GD}=0.07 b_{CA}=0.05 b_{IN}=0.03 b_{RC}=35.0	**0.014** **0.032** **12.1** **0.08** **0.05** **0.03** **37.6**	**93** **107** **93** **118** **101** **97** **107**

	M3	**-0.003**	**0.032**	E-E (Egypt) E-B (Egypt) C-A (China) U-S (UK) R-U(Russia) Total: 5 MFs	1.18 31.75 47.64 9.20 10.23	b_{RE}=0.015 b_{RI}=0.030 b_{AG}=13.0 b_{GD}=0.07 b_{CA}=0.05 b_{IN}=0.03 b_{RG}=35.0	**0.013** **0.031** **11.7** **0.08** **0.05** **0.03** **35.7**	**90** **102** **90** **113** **109** **110** **102**
	M4	**0.003**	**0.023**	E-B (Egypt) S-B (USA) C-A (China) Total: 3 MFs	91.09 0.50 8.41	b_{RE}=0.015 **b_{RI}=0.010** b_{AG}=13.0 b_{GD}=0.07 b_{CA}=0.05 b_{IN}=0.03 b_{RG}=35.0	**0.004** **0.017** **13.9** **0.02** **0.01** **0.04** **13.7**	**26** **174** **107** **26** **30** **132** **39**
Third: The models changing some factors' target values	M5	**-0.007**	**0.036**	E-B (Egypt) C-I (China) S-B (USA) Total: 3 MFs	14.04 75.92 10.03	b_{RE}=0.015 b_{RI}=0.030 b_{AG}=13.0 **b_{GD}=0.20** b_{CA}=0.05 b_{IN}=0.03 b_{RG}=35.0	**0.017** **0.032** **9.4** **0.13** **0.07** **0.02** **46.4**	**110** **107** **73** **67** **133** **68** **133**
	M6	**-0.005**	**0.037**	C-A (China) C-I (China) S-B (USA) Total: 3 MFs	57.02 8.75 34.23	b_{RE}=0.015 b_{RI}=0.030 b_{AG}=13.0 b_{GD}=0.07 b_{CA}=0.05 b_{IN}=0.03 **b_{RG}=70.0**	**0.017** **0.032** **13.0** **0.17** **0.04** **0.02** **56.8**	**111** **106** **100** **238** **81** **69** **81**
	M7	**-0.001**	**0.025**	E-E (Egypt) E-B (Egypt) K-C (KSA) C-I (China) C-A (China) Total: 5 MFs	23.19 39.35 22.29 12.50 2.67	b_{RE}=0.015 b_{RI}=0.030 b_{AG}=13.0 b_{GD}=0.07 b_{CA}=0.05 b_{IN}=0.03 **b_{RG}=10.0**	**0.006** **0.048** **12.9** **0.03** **0.08** **0.03** **16.1**	**39** **161** **99** **39** **161** **111** **161**

Table 7.11 shows the results for eight MinMax GP models, where the baseline model selects five mutual funds with a portfolio return of -0.003 and risk of 0.033. This portfolio gives a reasonable balance to achieving the seven factors involved with percentage achievements of 107% for RI, CA and RG, 93% for RE and AG, 117% for GD and 104% for IN.

M1 generates the same return with higher risk (with a portfolio of four mutual funds) even though it has higher weights for risk and return than the baseline model. M2 selects a portfolio of the same mutual funds as in the baseline portfolio, but with different proportions.

The return and risk are the same for both M2 and baseline portfolios. In M3, higher weights for risk and regional preferences are assigned and this provides a portfolio that is characterised by slightly lower risk at the same return level (consisting of five mutual funds), compared to the baseline model.

Furthermore, setting a challenging target value for the risk in M4 provides a portfolio that has a significantly lower risk and higher return, with a constituent of three mutual funds, compared to the baseline portfolio. This is at the expense of percentage achievement for other macroeconomic factors.

In M5, the target is to achieve more in one of the macroeconomic factors, namely GD, which produces a portfolio with lower return and higher risk compared to the baseline portfolio.

M6 gives a particular preference for the North America region where the model selects three mutual funds, of which one is from the preferred region, as the model tries to put together a portfolio that achieves all the targeted values of different factors.

This implies that the model could not find suitable mutual funds in one region to select from and complements the choice with other regions' mutual funds to achieve the overall balance between factors with reasonable return and risk.

M7, on the other hand, selects five mutual funds of which three are strictly from the targeted region (the MENA region) with an average return of -0.001 and a risk of 0.025, significantly better than the baseline results.

7.5 Analysis of Overall Results

7.5.1 Comparison of Relevant Portfolios

The following table sets out a comparison of the relevant portfolios.

Table 7.12: The return, risk and number of MFs in GP portfolios

GP Models	**Experiments**		Portfolios Analysis Criteria		
			Return	Risk	Number of MFs
Weighted GP Models	Baseline Model		**-0.003**	**0.030**	**6**
	Models changing the deviational variable weights	W1 High weights for RE, RI & AG	**-0.003**	**0.037**	**4**
		W2 High weights for GD, CA & IN	**-0.003**	**0.030**	**6**
		W3 High weights for RI & RG	**-0.003**	**0.030**	**6**
	Models changing some factor's target values	W4 Changed target for **RI**	**-0.004**	**0.025**	**5**
		W5 Changed target for **GD**	**-0.005**	**0.028**	**5**
		W6 Changed target for **RG** (70)	**-0.007**	**0.030**	**4**

		W7 Changed target for **RG** (10)	**0.001**	**0.024**	**4**
Lexicographic GP Models	Baseline Model		**-0.004**	**0.034**	**4**
	Models changing the deviational variable weights	L1 RE, RI & AG are in the 1st priority level	**-0.004**	**0.034**	**4**
		L2 GD, CA & IN are in the 1st priority level	**-0.003**	**0.030**	**6**
		L3 RI & RG in the 1st priority level	**-0.003**	**0.030**	**6**
	Models changing some factor's target values	L4 Changed target for **RI**	**0.004**	**0.023**	**1**
		L5 Changed target for **GD**	**-0.005**	**0.032**	**4**
		L6 Changed target for **RG** (70)	**-0.005**	**0.032**	**4**
		L7 Changed target for **RG** (10)	**-0.004**	**0.034**	**4**
MinMax (Chebyshev) GP Models	Baseline Model		**-0.003**	**0.033**	**5**
	Models changing the deviational variable weights	M1 High weights for RE, RI & AG	**-0.003**	**0.036**	**4**
		M2 High weights for GD, CA & IN	**-0.003**	**0.033**	**5**
		M3 High weights for RI & RG	**-0.003**	**0.032**	**5**
	Models changing some factor's target values	M4 Change the target for **RI**	**0.003**	**0.023**	**3**
		M5 Change the target for **GD**	**-0.007**	**0.036**	**3**
		M6 Change the target for **RG** (70)	**-0.005**	**0.037**	**3**
		M7 Change the target for **RG** (10)	**-0.001**	**0.025**	**5**
-	**EW** (Hypothetical Equally-Weighted Portfolio)		**-0.004**	**0.020**	**20**

Table 7.12 gives the return, risk, and the number of mutual funds for all the experimental models in this chapter. The WGP baseline portfolio has the lowest risk compared to the LGP and MinMax GP baseline portfolios. L1 has slightly better risk than W1 and M1, while it has lower return.

Comparing W1, L1 and M1 (which are experiments that give higher weight or priority to MF specific factors) with their respective baseline models, there are no improvements in returns, which are associated with higher risks.

The models that give more weight or a higher priority level to the macroeconomic factors are W2, L2 and M2, where the results for W2 and L2 are almost identical, while it is different (with higher risk) in the corresponding M2 model. Further, W3 and L3 are nearly identical in their results with a return of -0.003 and a risk of 0.030 in both models as they assign higher weights or higher priority to the risks and regional factors. Model M3 selects a portfolio that has a similar return compared to W3 and L2, though with higher risk.

W4, L4 and M4 have a target value of 0.01 for risk, which is lower than the world average in this experiment. The three models succeed in attaining the lowest risk for the selected portfolio compared to all the experimental models in this chapter. L4, however, has the highest return over W4 and M4.

W5, L5 and M5 give a high target value for the GD factor and select a portfolio from three to five mutual funds. The L5 portfolio has a higher return compared to M5, but same return compared to W5. The lowest risk amongst the three of them is in W5.

W6, L6 and M6 try to select their portfolios based on a high preference for the North America region. W6 has the lowest return, while L6 and M6 have the same return (although higher than W6's return) with the lowest risk in W6 compared to L6 and M6. The models' results and the aggregated comparison seem to imply that the preference for such a region does not generate a reasonable performance for the selected portfolios.

W7 and M7, on the other hand, generate better returns and risk compared to their respective baseline models and in fact compared to many of the other models. However, L7 produces the same return and risk as its baseline model. This result seems to imply that the preference given to that region is effective, as the models were able find a good fit for all the factors while also selecting a portfolio that generates better return and risk levels (or at least the same level as the respective baseline, as in L7).

Finally, comparing all the portfolios selected in this chapter with a hypothetical portfolio (consisting of twenty mutual funds equally weighted, called EW in table 7.12) shows that using any GP model for selecting international mutual funds is significantly better. GP models select fewer numbers of mutual funds for the portfolios. The GP portfolios perform better not only in terms of risk-adjusted returns, but also in terms of the transaction and investment costs.

7.5.2 Redundancy Issues in LGP

Redundancy of goals in LGP is not only a theoretical possibility but a practical problem. Usually redundancy occurs due to one or more of the following reasons (Tamiz, Jones and Romero, 1998):

- Fixing the target values equal to or close to the ideal values (optimistic values in this context).
- Setting an excessive number of priority levels, especially compared to the number of goals.
- Including many two-sided goals in the achievement function. These are goals in which both deviational variables (negative and positive) are penalised.

The redundancy problem does not occur, however, in this chapter's experiments with LGP, since the priority levels, target values and penalisation of the unwanted deviational variables are all set realistically and reasonably.

However, if investors or decision makers want to set optimistic target values or assign many priority levels based on their preferences, the redundancy issue may occur and should be tested for.

For example, if an investor requires the target value for risk or inflation to be significantly lower than the world average, the resulting models could well face a redundancy issue.

In fact, upon carrying out further experiments with the target value for RE set at 0.02 (which is 100% higher than the average and 50% higher than the target value for experiments reported in this chapter), the resulting solutions indicate a redundancy issue with priority level 2.

The following table illustrates the resulting portfolios return, risk and constituents after re-running the LGP models with RE=0.02.

Table 7.13: The resulting portfolios of re-running LGP models with RE=0.02

LGP Models with RE=0.02 *(LGP models are called LLk (where k = 1, ... ,8), corresponding to the 8 LGP experiments in table 7.10)*	Return	Risk	Selected Mutual Funds		% of achievement for each target value for the 7 factors		
			MFs (Country)	Proportions (%)	b_i	Achieved	%
LL1	**-0.005**	**0.038**	C-A (China) S-B (USA) Total: 2 MFs	65.06 34.94	b_{RE}=0.02 b_{RI}=0.03 b_{AG}=13.0 b_{GD}=0.07 b_{CA}=0.05 b_{IN}=0.03 b_{RG}=35.0	0.017 0.032 13.0 0.17 0.04 0.02 57.0	84 106 100 238 79 70 163

LL2	-0.004	0.035	E-B (Egypt) C-A (China) S-B (USA) Total: 3 MFs	11.86 58.13 30.01	**b_{RE}=0.02** **b_{RI}=0.03** **b_{AG}=13.0** **b_{GD}=0.07** **b_{CA}=0.05** **b_{IN}=0.03** **b_{RG}=35.0**	0.015 0.030 13.0 0.15 0.04 0.02 51.3	76 100 100 210 74 78 146
LL3	-0.003	0.030	E-E (Egypt) E-B (Egypt) K-C (KSA) C-A (China) U-S (UK) R-U (Russia) Total: 6 MFs	1.13 35.09 2.23 43.18 13.51 4.86	b_{RE}=0.02 b_{RI}=0.03 b_{AG}=13.0 b_{GD}=0.07 b_{CA}=0.05 b_{IN}=0.03 b_{RG}=35.0	0.012 0.030 13.0 0.07 0.05 0.03 35.0	61 100 100 104 100 100 100
LL4	-0.003	0.030	E-E (Egypt) E-B (Egypt) K-C (KSA) C-A (China) U-S (UK) R-U (Russia) Total: 6 MFs	1.13 35.09 2.23 43.18 13.51 4.86	b_{RE}=0.02 b_{RI}=0.03 b_{AG}=13.0 b_{GD}=0.07 b_{CA}=0.05 b_{IN}=0.03 b_{RG}=35.0	0.012 0.030 13.0 0.07 0.05 0.03 35.0	61 100 100 104 100 100 100
LL5	0.004	0.023	E-B (Egypt) Total: 1 MF	100	b_{RE}=0.02 **b_{RI}=0.01** b_{AG}=13.0 b_{GD}=0.07 b_{CA}=0.05 b_{IN}=0.03 b_{RG}=35.0	0.002 0.015 14.8 0.00 0.00 0.04 10.0	10 153 114 8 16 140 29
LL6	-0.005	0.038	C-A (China) S-B (USA) Total: 2 MFs	65.06 34.94	b_{RE}=0.02 b_{RI}=0.01 b_{AG}=13.0 **b_{GD}=0.20** b_{CA}=0.05 b_{IN}=0.03 b_{RG}=35.0	0.017 0.032 13.0 0.17 0.04 0.02 57.0	84 106 100 83 79 70 163
LL7	-0.005	0.038	C-A (China) S-B (USA) Total: 2 MFs	65.06 34.94	b_{RE}=0.02 b_{RI}=0.03 b_{AG}=13.0 b_{GD}=0.07 b_{CA}=0.05 b_{IN}=0.03 **b_{RG}=70.0**	0.015 0.030 13.0 0.15 0.04 0.02 51.3	84 106 100 238 79 70 81
LL8	-0.005	0.038	C-A (China) S-B (USA) Total: 2 MFs	65.06 34.94	b_{RE}=0.02 b_{RI}=0.03 b_{AG}=13.0 b_{GD}=0.07 b_{CA}=0.05 b_{IN}=0.03 **b_{RG}=10.0**	0.015 0.030 13.0 0.15 0.04 0.02 51.3	84 106 100 238 79 70 570

Table 7.13 shows the results for the LGP models with the RE target value set at an optimistic level of 0.02. Redundancy reported for the models LL1, LL2, LL7 and LL8 in priority level 2—i.e., the objectives in priority level 2—can be ignored completely. This means that the LL1, LL2, LL7 and LL8 portfolios reported in table 7.13 are the result of the objectives in priority level 1 only. Thus, the results do not reflect the decision maker's preferences as represented by two priority levels.

7.6 Conclusion and Further Remarks

This chapter explores portfolio selection models using different GP variants with applications to mutual funds across the globe. The WGP models are reasonable in reflecting the investor's preferences. In particular, WGP models show how different weighting and target values for various factors could result in different portfolios.

However, if the investor prefers certain factors over others with significant distinction in their priorities, LGP models would be more suitable. With LGP, the investor can group the unwanted deviational variables in certain priority levels, indicating that achieving the objectives in the higher priority level is infinitely more important than achieving the objectives in the lower priority level. Care has to be taken in setting realistic target values, since assigning over-optimistic target values may result in redundancy in LGP.

MinMax GP models for portfolio selection serve as a compromise in terms of achieving several factors in one model. MinMax GP is well-known for giving fair solutions (Romero, 1991). Hence, if the investor is interested in achieving many factors concurrently with or without weighting preferences, MinMax GP is a suitable model.

The three groups of models, namely WGP, LGP and MinMax GP, are practical in terms of reflecting the investor's various preferences. In some experiments, the three models succeed in achieving the ultimate goal but with some variations. For instance, experiments W4, L4 and M4 have a target value of 0.01 for risk, which is lower than the world average, challenging the models to achieve lower risk than the normal case. The three models succeed in reaching the lowest risk for the selected portfolios compared not only to their respective baseline models, but also compared to all the experimental models in this chapter. However, there are some differences within each model's results, most notably in percentage achievements of factors and the number of mutual funds selected.

In WGP models of W2 (higher weights for GD, CA and IN) and W3 (higher weights for RI and RG) similar portfolios are selected compared to their baseline model. This seems to imply that the macroeconomic factors in W2 are already taken care of in the baseline model. The same applies to W3 (risk and regional preferences), where there is no possibility for further improvements and hence the model selects the same portfolio as that of the baseline.

The bottom line result from this chapter is that using any GP model for selecting an investor's portfolio produces better performing portfolios compared to a merely equal-weighted portfolio of available mutual funds, in terms of risk, return and investment costs involved (as discussed in section 7.5.1).

Furthermore, many researchers recommend investing a portion of investors' portfolios in global mutual funds in order to obtain better-performing portfolios through diversification (for instance, Redman, Gullett and Manakyan, 2000). However, investing in international mutual funds requires significant time and effort in selecting amongst them. Therefore, the success of an international mutual fund portfolio depends partly on the ability of the total portfolio to generate risk-adjusted returns equal to or greater than the domestic stock market index, as well as the ability of the total portfolio to generate returns better than those of domestic mutual funds. Since this chapter experiments with international mutual funds portfolio selection from ten countries, investors from each of the ten countries could compare the performance of the portfolios selected in this chapter against the performance of their domestic market index or domestic mutual funds for sound investing decisions. For instance, if an investor is based in the UK, the comparison should be with UK's market index, i.e., FTSE 100, where the return during the testing time period is -0.005 with a total risk of 0.027, whereas the return on the UK's mutual funds (the two included in this chapter's experiments) is -0.005 with a standard deviation of 0.029. Both comparisons are favourable to many of portfolios selected in this chapter as they produce better returns with reasonable risks.

Based on the conclusions reached, it is essential for an investor or a decision maker to define goals and objectives clearly in order to obtain the most suitable solution to a given problem. Considering an extended set of factors concurrently, preferring some factors over others, having a clear distinction in factors' importance by setting priorities, and the choice of the set of deviational variables to penalise, representing more is better, less is better, or neither, are all examples of the ways an investor could utilise GP models for solving portfolio selection problems.

Therefore, the results obtained in this chapter, although promising, are not conclusive, since they are based on certain factors, target values, priority levels, time periods and a specific set of penalised unwanted deviational variables. One way to validate the results obtained from the experiments is to include other factors, different target values, other priority levels, different time periods and other sets of penalised unwanted deviational variables.

In particular, similar experiments could be carried out in further research by replacing the extended factors set in this chapter with the set of factors described in Arbitrage Pricing Theory (Ross, 1976), for example. Also, the three factors model of Fama and French (1993) could be experimented with in future studies using this chapter's scientific framework for testing an extended set of factors.

Fama and French (1993) note that stock-market factors include overall market factor and factors related to firm size and book-to-market equity. They also highlight two bond-market factors which are related to maturity and default risks. Therefore, potential extended factors for further research could include such factors as those described by the three-factors model of Fama and French or the APT model, with similar or different time periods, financial assets, etc.

Furthermore, the results reported in this chapter are only relevant for mutual fund portfolio selection and analysis. Further research may want to explore the potential of the GP extended factors model for global stocks. In particular, further research could investigate different criteria, other markets, and model parameters for stocks in global markets.

It is also essential for investors to define the relevant values for their decision making. Keeney (2003) comments that values are more fundamental to a decision problem than alternatives. Values are principles used for evaluation. They are used to evaluate the actual or potential consequences of action and inaction, of proposed alternatives, and of decisions. They rank from important principles that must be upheld to guidelines for preferences among choices. Periodically, a decision maker should examine their achievements in terms of his/her values and ask if they can do better. Therefore, it is important in any portfolio selection problem to first decide what the decision maker wants and then figure out how to get it.

A potential investor could benefit from the results obtained in this chapter's experiments by selecting portfolios that incorporate factors that characterise today's world to impact their investment performance favourably.

CHAPTER EIGHT

PERSPECTIVES ON INVESTMENT DECISION MAKING AND PORTFOLIO SELECTION USING GOAL PROGRAMMING

This book provides practitioners with a new and superior scientific framework for investment decision making, while aiming to stimulate further research and development by academics.

A comprehensive review of existing literature on Goal Programming features used for portfolio selection is provided, and one reason for the success of GP is found to be its underlying satisficing philosophy.

New GP models are developed and extensions to some of the reviewed models are offered. Thorough testing and analysis are then carried out. In particular, the book explores selecting portfolios of mutual funds both in a developed market (i.e., UK), and in an emerging market (i.e., Egypt). Three techniques are offered for setting up portfolios of mutual funds, in which the performance comparison of the selected portfolios reveals that the mutual fund portfolios constructed, based on Sharpe and Goal Programming, have the minimum deviations from each other as well as compared to the relevant benchmarks. Although the Sharpe and Treynor methodologies of ranking and selecting the best mutual funds are well established historically, it is found that the GP methodology performs at least as well as both Sharpe and Treynor, especially when compared with relevant benchmarks. The results also seem to suggest that the use of GP is as practical in crisis time (the experiment in the UK financial market) as in regular time (the experiment in Egypt's financial market). This result is critical, as the spread of the current financial and economic crisis has challenged many of the key assumptions of modern finance, including that of efficient markets and market allocations of risk.

The book also explores the portfolio selection problem with applications to stocks. The performance comparison between the stock portfolios reveals that the portfolio constructed based on GP has the minimum deviation relative to the benchmark. It would be interesting for further research, and possible validation of results, to run the same experiments using different markets and/or time periods for mutual funds, stocks, or even other investment instruments.

Building on the results of selecting portfolios of both mutual funds and stocks using the Goal Programming, Sharpe and Treynor approaches, further research to explore the selection of different types of assets in one portfolio can be easily carried out, possibly with different types of mutual funds, stocks, bonds, derivatives, etc.

In exploring the portfolio selection problems, several weighting schemes for selecting portfolio proportions for mutual funds and stocks are investigated. The weighting schemes comparisons show that using an optimisation methodology produces more reasonable portfolio proportions when considering both risk and return. This is followed by the Sharpe and Treynor methodologies which measure the risk-adjusted returns.

The book proposes and examines many weighting schemes, which investors may wish to explore systematically in order to establish their preferred proportions for investment portfolios. From an academic point of view, it is hoped that some of the weighting schemes experimented with in this book will assist in stimulating further research and innovation in obtaining systematic ways for deciding on portfolio constituents' proportions.

Risk-return based portfolio selection, although well known, has been questioned in terms of its applicability in today's complex and changing world. Therefore, this book explores portfolio selection models using an extended set of factors with applications to mutual funds across the world. Different GP variants are used in these experiments, containing seven factors, under the headings of mutual-funds specific, macroeconomic factors, and regional preferences.

The results of the extended factor models for portfolio selection seem to provide reasonable support for the underlying philosophy of the GP variants. In particular, WGP is found to be suitable for reflecting the preferences of investors by setting appropriate weights for the unwanted deviational variables. LGP is more relevant for investors who wish to further prioritise the achievement of unwanted deviational variables. The fairness of the solution of MinMax GP is also supported as it serves as a compromise in terms of achieving several factors with different weights in one model.

Overall, the WGP, LGP and MinMax GP models, as applied in the experiments with extended factors, are found to offer practical approaches in reflecting the investor's various preferences in the resulting portfolios. In some of the experiments the models succeed in achieving the ultimate goal but with some variations. For instance, they succeed in reaching the lowest risk for the selected portfolios compared to their respective baseline models, as well as compared to some other experimental models. However, there are some differences within each model's results, most notably in percentage achievements of other factors, and in the number of mutual funds selected.

The bottom line result from investigating extended factors is that using any GP model for selecting an investor's portfolio produces better-performing portfolios compared to a mere equal weight portfolio of available mutual funds, in terms of risk, return and implicit investment costs. In addition, the success of an international mutual fund portfolio depends partly on the ability of the total portfolio to generate risk-adjusted returns equal to or greater than the domestic stock market index, or at least better than those of domestic mutual funds. The book reports relevant comparisons in one of the ten markets experimented with for selecting an international mutual fund portfolio, with favourable results.

The experiments on weighting schemes together with the experiments on the extended factors for mutual funds portfolio selection using GP can be extended for further research. For example, the twenty mutual funds across the world could be selected using a different criterion and then used in weighting scheme experiments. Similarly, the extended factors could be explored with more factors or with other regions, etc. Furthermore, other risk measures, which are discussed throughout the book, could be used within the experiments as factors to be investigated for their impact on portfolio selection. Alternatively, such risk measures could be used as part of evaluation criteria for the resulting portfolios.

The book, in general, strives to provide both practitioners and academics with a scientific approach to portfolio selection using goal programming which is capable of achieving a required set of preferences.

Based on the conclusions reached throughout this book, it is highly advisable for investors or decision makers to clearly define their goals and objectives in order to obtain the most suitable solution to their given problems. Amongst these considerations for example are:

- The choice of appropriate deviational variables to penalise, representing more is better, less is better, or neither.
- The concurrent ranking of extended factors, preferring some factors over others and making a clear distinction in factors' importance by setting priorities.

A potential investor could benefit from the results of the experiments reported in this book by selecting portfolios that incorporate factors that characterise today's world to impact their investment performance favourably. Moreover, the book provides scientific approaches for portfolio selection with goal programming which it is hoped will provide added-value for practitioners in complementing their financial expertise with a sound scientific decision-making framework.

It is worth emphasising that the data used for the portfolio selection models in the book are publicly and freely available. However, practitioners (either investors or policy makers) usually have access to an extra wealth of information and more accurate data on their investments. The experiments hence can be repeated utilising such additional data with potentials for further improvements in their results.

It is hoped that the issues discussed in this book and their outcomes will start a new avenue of research into the applications of GP and its variants for portfolio selection. The experiments carried out and the results reported in this book, although promising, are not conclusive, since they are based on a specific set of defined parameters. Therefore, further research is warranted to explore similar or different experiments with another set of parameters.

In particular, the experiments are based on certain factors, target values, priority levels, time periods and a specific set of penalised unwanted deviational variables. One way to validate the results obtained from the experiments is to include other factors, different target values, other priority levels, different time periods and other sets of penalised unwanted deviational variables. A potential set of factors could include the factors described in the three factors model or the Arbitrage Pricing Theory Model, amongst others.

It is further hoped that disseminating the findings of this book will stimulate discussions within the relevant communities with a view to extend the state-of-the-art of portfolio analysis in research and practice to new horizons.

In any case, the usefulness and flexibility of the use of Goal Programming models for portfolio selection means that such models remain promising. The book has shown that the Goal Programming models for portfolio selection are characterised by simplicity of form, practicality of approach and sound performance.

CHAPTER NINE

PRACTICAL THOUGHTS FOR FUTURE WORK

9.1 General thoughts

Real-world decision problems are usually changeable, complex and resist treatment with conventional approaches. Therefore, traditional quantitative modelling for portfolio and risk management that relies on simplifying real-world problems to find an ideal (most probably non-practical) solution is no longer valid for handling today's challenges.

In a post-crisis world, professional investors are searching for higher returns in riskier assets and a lower risk through well-diversified portfolios. However, the key question is whether the capacity of investment institutions to take into account relevant risk factors has grown at the same pace as their rapid asset allocation diversification. The recent financial crisis exposed portfolios to new risks that had not been widely anticipated.

This chapter highlights and suggests unconventional approaches to risk management that could be utilised within the investment decision-making approach of Goal Programming. The risk is addressed by suggesting some key views which should be considered in identifying, measuring and mitigating risk in a post-crisis context.

Risk and portfolio management issues could be soundly addressed amid today's challenges by a quantitative approach utilising Goal Programming in order to find a practical and real-world solution to an investment problem, rather than an idealistic or optimal solution to a highly simplified model of that problem.

9.2 Addressing Risks

Risk-management practices have become a central topic since the recent financial crisis. In broad terms, risk management is about maximising the probability of achieving certain objectives on the investment horizon while staying within a risk budget.

Risk management is no longer a compliance issue. Organisations/ investors should identify and prepare for non-preventable risks that arise externally to their investment strategy.

Risk management, in a post-crisis context, starts with understanding qualitative distinctions among the three main risks, namely: preventable risk, unpreventable risk, and strategy risk.

- Preventable risk is basically internal risks that should be prevented. These arise within the organisation and therefore could be controlled and should be avoided or eliminated.
- Unpreventable risks usually arise from events outside the organisation and beyond its control. These could be identified as external risks, which call for another approach to their management. Because organisations cannot prevent such risks/ events from occurring, their management must focus on identification and mitigation of their impacts.
- Strategy risk cannot be managed according to the methods used for preventable or unpreventable risks, due to its different nature. This type of risk needs a risk-management system designed to reduce the probability that the assumed risks actually materialise and to improve the organisation's ability to manage or contain the risk events should they occur.

Many investment professionals, in both public- and private-sector organisations, used Modern Portfolio Theory to establish and maintain the portfolios of their funds in the relatively calm post–World War II environment. Today's world is far more complex, changeable and volatile, and is characterised by interconnectedness. The following are the key points to consider in risk management in a post-crisis context:

- Managing risk is very different from managing strategy. Risk management focuses on the negatives (threats or failures) rather than opportunities and successes.
- A new investment strategy is needed, one that places risk first in its multitude of dimensions.
- Risk was either improperly measured, or considered a distant second to return. This now needs to change—forever.
- Risk metrics based on volatility, such as Value at Risk, are inherently short-term, making them unsuitable for institutional investors or long-term investors.
- Risk-factor analysis is critical to any institutional investor in order to identify underlying investment risk factors that describe the return variation in a particular portfolio or asset.

The above are a few examples of how to consider risk in investment portfolios. Utilising Goal Programming for measuring and mitigating risks would be of practical benefit if further developed to consider various other factors of relevance. These and other thoughts should be further developed in future work.

APPENDICES

Appendix A

Table (A-1): The names of the mutual funds used in chapter four's experiments

The Mutual Funds in UK's Financial Market			The Mutual Funds in Egypt's Financial Market		
No.	MF Abbreviation	Mutual Fund Name	No.	MF Abbreviation	Mutual Fund Name
1	AI	**Aberdeen Income Fund ICVC- Alpha Income Fund**	1	AE	**American Express Bank I MF**
2	AR	**Allianz RCM UK Equity Fund**	2	AM	**Arab Misr Insurance Group MF**
			3	BA	**Bank of Alexandria MF**
3	AN	**Aviva Investors UK Growth & Value Fund**	4	BC	**Banque du Caire MF**
			5	B1	**Banque Misr I MF**
4	FC	**F&C Investment Funds ICVC -UK Opportunities F.**	6	B2	**Banque Misr II MF**
			7	DM	**Delta Mutual Fund**
5	FI	**Fidelity Investment Funds ICVC- Special Situations Fund**	8	EA	**Egyptian American Bank MF**
			9	EG	**Egyptian Gulf Bank MF**
6	GA	**GAM Funds- UK Diversified Fund**	10	ED	**Export Development Bank MF**
			11	ME	**Misr Exterior Bank MF**
7	HE	**Henderson UK & Europe Funds- UK Opportunities Fund**	12	MI	**Misr International Bank MF**
			13	MR	**Misr Iran Development Bank MF**
8	II	**Insight Investment Discretionary Funds ICVC- UK Equity Fund**	14	N1	**National Bank of Egypt I MF**
			15	N2	**National Bank of Egypt II MF**

9	JP	**JPM Life Ltd- UK Disciplined (350) Equity Fund**	16	OT	**Orient Trust MF**
			17	S1	**Societe Arab Int'l Banque I MF**
10	SU	**Skandia UK Best Ideas Fund**	18	S2	**Societe Arab Int'l Banque II MF**
			19	SC	**Suez Canal Bank MF**

Appendix B

Table (A-2): The names of the stocks used in chapter five's experiments

10 stocks from FTSE 100 of UK's Financial Market	
Stock Abbreviation	**Stocks Name**
HS	**HSBC**
TR	**Thomson Reuters**
PE	**Pearson**
BH	**BHP Billiton**
UN	**Unilever**
RT	**Rio Tinto**
RD	**Royal Dutch Shell**
VO	**Vodafone**
GS	**GlaxoSmithKline**
LB	**Lloyds Banking Group**

Appendix C

Table (A-3): The names of the mutual funds and stocks used in experiments reported in chapter six

The Mutual Funds and Stocks used in the Weighting Schemes Experiments					
No.	MF Abbreviation	**Mutual Fund Name**	No.	Stock Abbreviation	**Stock Name**
1	AI	**Aberdeen Income Fund ICVC- Alpha Income Fund**	1	HS	**HSBC**
2	AR	**Allianz RCM UK Equity Fund**	2	TR	**Thomson Reuters**
3	AN	**Aviva Investors UK Growth & Value Fund**	3	PE	**Pearson**
4	FC	**F&C Investment Funds ICVC -UK Opportunities Fund**	4	BH	**BHP Billiton**
5	FI	**Fidelity Investment Funds ICVC- Special Situations Fund**	5	UN	**Unilever**
6	GA	**GAM Funds- UK Diversified Fund**	6	RT	**Rio Tinto**
7	HE	**Henderson UK & Europe Funds- UK Opportunities Fund**	7	RD	**Royal Dutch Shell**
8	II	**Insight Investment Discretionary Funds ICVC- UK Equity Fund**	8	VO	**Vodafone**
9	JP	**JPM Life Ltd- UK Disciplined (350) Equity Fund**	9	GS	**GlaxoSmithKline**
10	SU	**Skandia UK Best Ideas Fund**	10	LB	**Lloyds Banking Group**

Appendix D

Table (A-4): The names of the mutual funds used in chapter seven's experiments

Region	Country	Mutual Fund Abbreviation	**Mutual Fund Name**
Middle East & North Africa (MENA)	Egypt	E-E	**EFG-Hermes-Bank Alexandria MF 1**
		E-B	**Banque Misr 1**
	KSA	K-C	**CAAM Saudi Fransi-Saudi Istithmar Equity Fund**
		K-S	**Saudi Hollandi Bank-Saudi Equity Trading Fund**
Asia Pacific	Japan	J-S	**SG Target Japan Fund**
		J-B	**BlackRock Japan Small Cap**
	China	C-A	**China AMC large-cap Select Fund**
		C-I	**China International Alpha Equity Fund**
Central Asia	India	I-R	**Reliance Vision Fund**
		I-B	**Birla Sun Life Equity Fund**
Western Europe	UK	U-A	**Allianz RCM UK Equity Fund**
		U-S	**Scottish Widows UK Equity Income Fund**
	Italy	T-I	**Imi-Italy**
		T-F	**Fondersel Italia**
Eastern Europe	Russia	R-S	**Solid Index MICEX-Open-End Fund**
		R-U	**Univer-Equity Fund Investments Fund**
North America	USA	S-B	**BlackRock Exchange Portfolio-Open-End Fund**
		S-A	**Barclays S&P 500 Stock Fund**
Latin America	Brazil	B-R	**Real FIA Dividendos**
		B-F	**FIA Mistyque-Open-End Fund**

Appendix E

Figure (A-5): A snapshot of one of the spreadsheets for the experiments in chapter four of this book

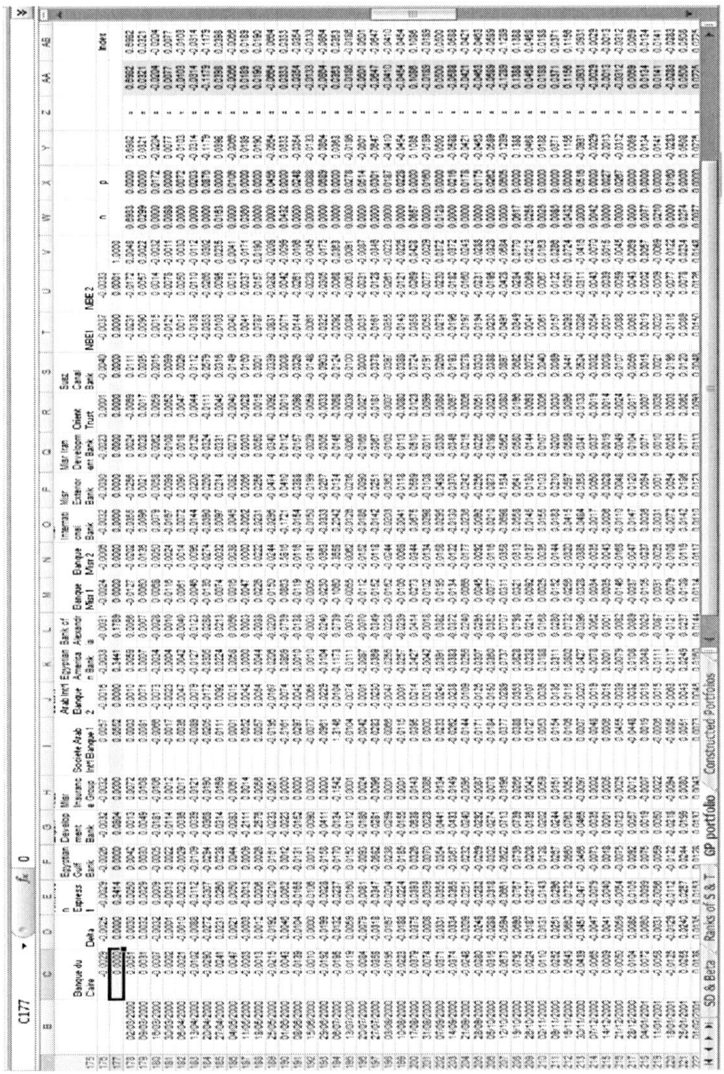

Appendix F

Figure (A-6): A snapshot of one of the spreadsheets for the experiments in chapter five of this book

I26 =AVERAGE(I6:I25)

	A	B	C	D	E	F	G	H	I	J	K	L
2												
3		The best 5 stocks based on Sharpe Ranking, are listed below:										
4		Sharpe Ranking	1	2	3	4	5					
5	Testing Period	Stock Name	Thomson Reuters	Lloyds Banking Group	Rio Tinto	BHP Billiton	Royal Dutch Shell		Sharpe Portfolio			Index
6	February 13, 2009	Returns	-0.02503	-0.41524	0.01671	-0.04270	0.03222		-0.0999780			-0.0238
7	February 20, 2009		-0.07356	-0.08308	-0.09008	-0.09859	-0.07688		-0.0834199			-0.0717
8	February 27, 2009		0.08614	0.03553	-0.00535	-0.03993	-0.07076		0.0339550			-0.0151
9	March 6, 2009		-0.03862	-0.27953	0.01345	0.04521	-0.02965		-0.0621148			-0.0781
10	March 13, 2009		0.07102	0.11441	0.13802	0.15744	0.08333		0.1091636			0.06314
11	March 20, 2009		0.04555	0.18153	-0.02332	0.08072	-0.02628		0.0653663			0.02375
12	March 27, 2009		-0.01730	0.37597	0.22209	-0.02559	0.03094		0.1084981			0.01457
13	April 3, 2009		0.09518	0.04075	0.00489	0.02271	-0.03129		0.0525465			0.03355
14	April 10, 2009		-0.01667	0.00390	-0.05202	-0.02290	-0.06790		-0.0206441			-0.0114
15	April 17, 2009		0.03753	0.31572	0.01590	-0.00355	-0.00919		0.0824909			0.02738
16	April 24, 2009		-0.00583	-0.04401	0.12317	0.02281	0.09850		0.0171205			0.01543
17	May 1, 2009		0.02700	0.09597	0.05798	-0.00070	0.00845		0.0419371			0.02098
18	May 8, 2009		-0.00743	-0.08120	0.05225	0.07043	0.04381		0.0037890			0.05158
19	May 18, 2009		-0.03339	-0.09211	-0.11183	-0.08143	-0.01235		-0.0696397			-0.0255
20	May 22, 2009		0.00298	0.00719	0.03955	0.00851	0.02188		0.0120538			0.00395
21	May 29, 2009		0.00297	-0.00875	0.01137	0.03797	0.02446		0.0088091			0.01206
22	June 5, 2009		0.02131	-0.02647	0.07177	0.05352	0.02507		0.0273956			0.00466
23	June 12, 2009		0.00406	-0.01360	0.03832	-0.04502	-0.02155		-0.0021223			0.00076
24	June 19, 2009		-0.03464	0.07198	-0.18609	-0.05320	-0.04286		-0.0458196			-0.0216
25	June 26, 2009		0.03289	-0.05014	-0.01671	-0.03592	-0.06095		-0.0068952			-0.0241
26								Average Return:	0.87%	Total Risk	0.060	
27												
28		Proportions	41.06%	20.48%	19.49%	18.70%	0.26%	100%				
29												
30												
31		Sharpe Index	0.04729	-0.41744	-0.43976	-0.45766	-0.87416					

Price | Sharpe | Treynor | GP

Appendix G

Figure (A-7): A snapshot of one of the spreadsheets for the experiments in chapter six of this book

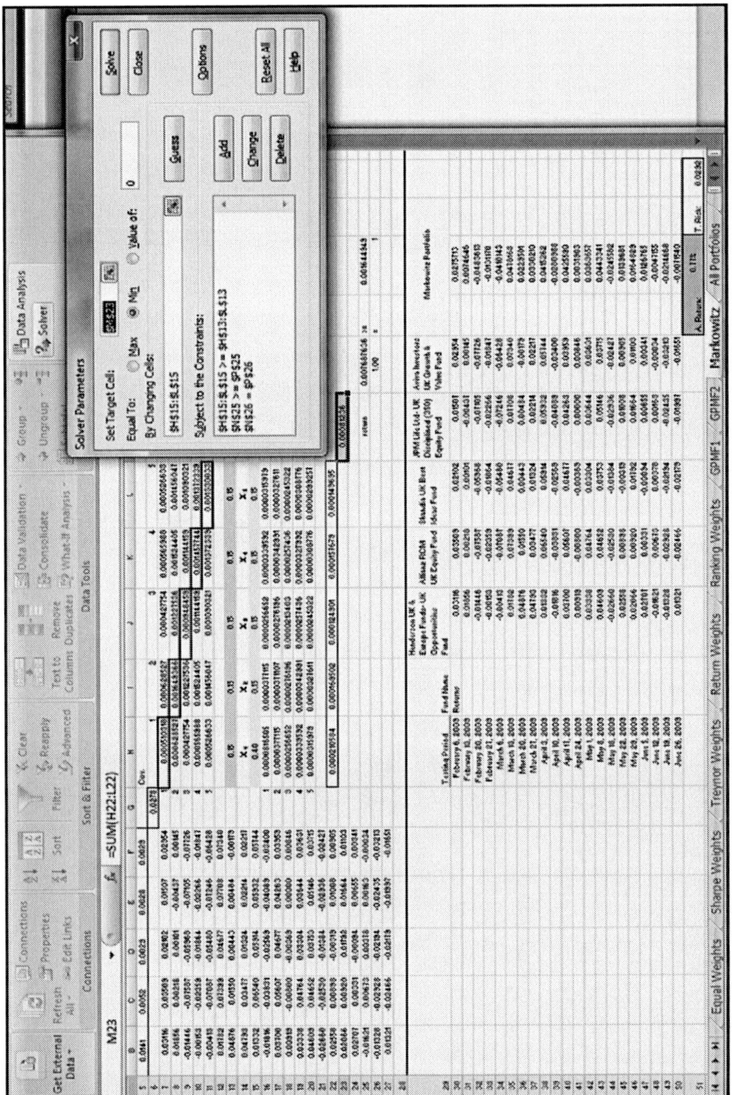

Appendix H

Figure (A-8): A snapshot of one of the WGP experiments in chapter seven of this book

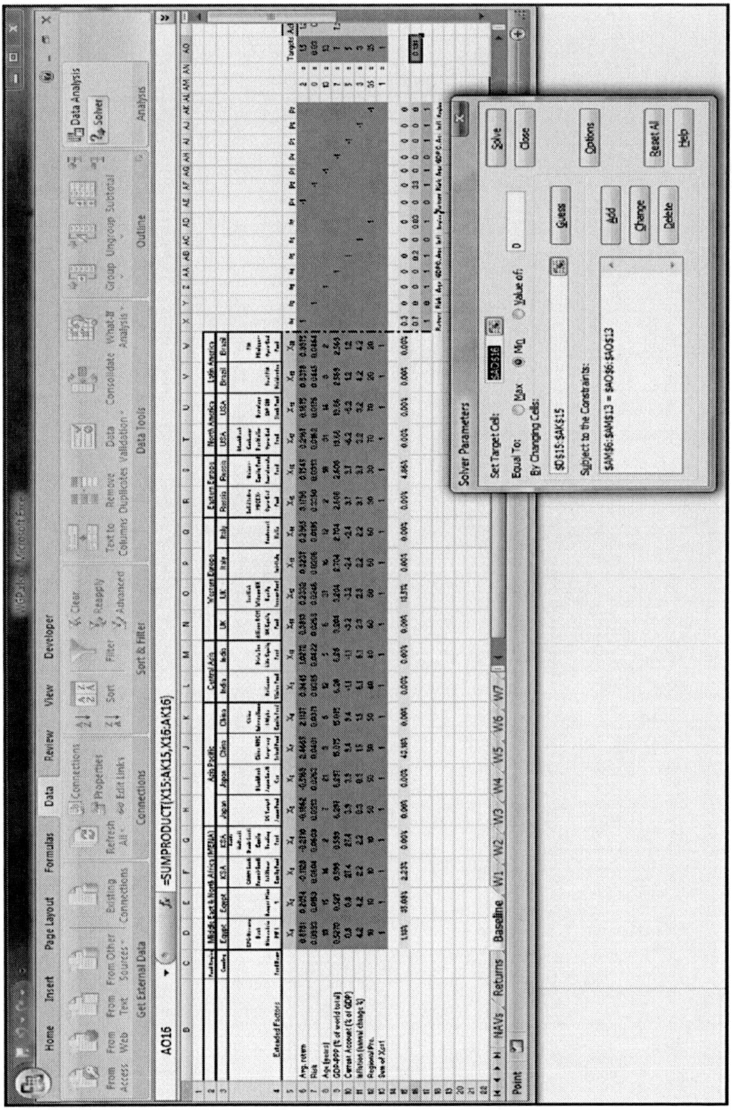

Appendix I

Figure (A-9): A snapshot of one of the LGP experiments in chapter seven of this book

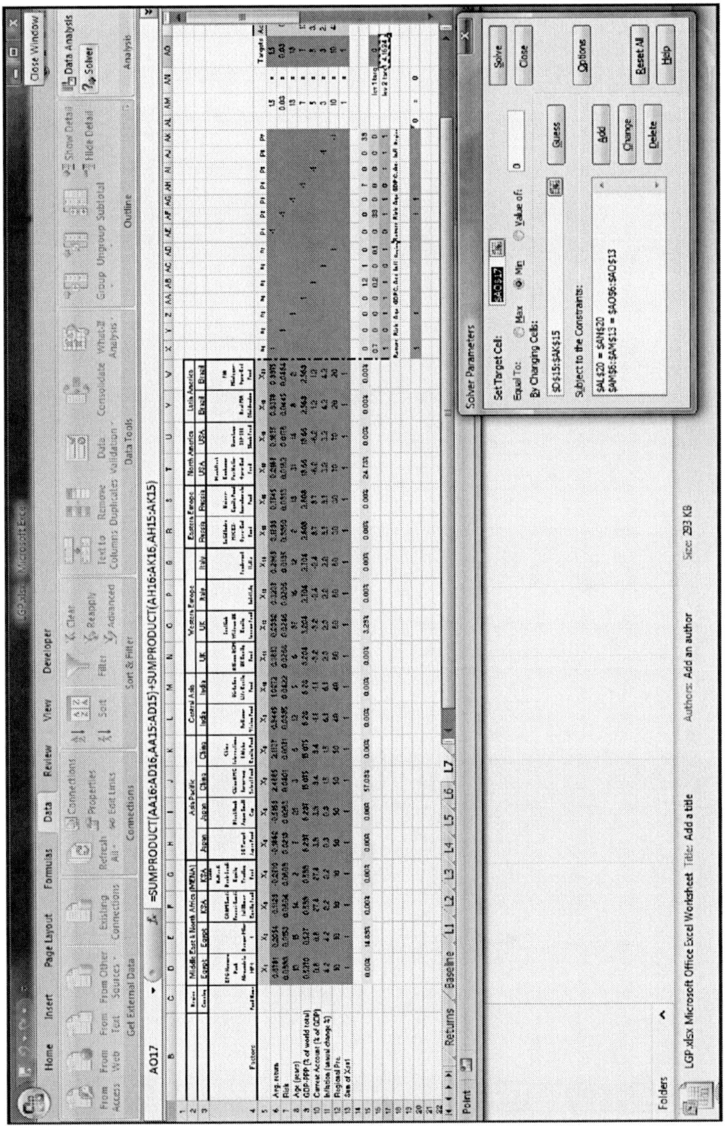

Appendix J

Figure (A-10): A snapshot of one of the MinMax GP experiments in chapter seven of this book

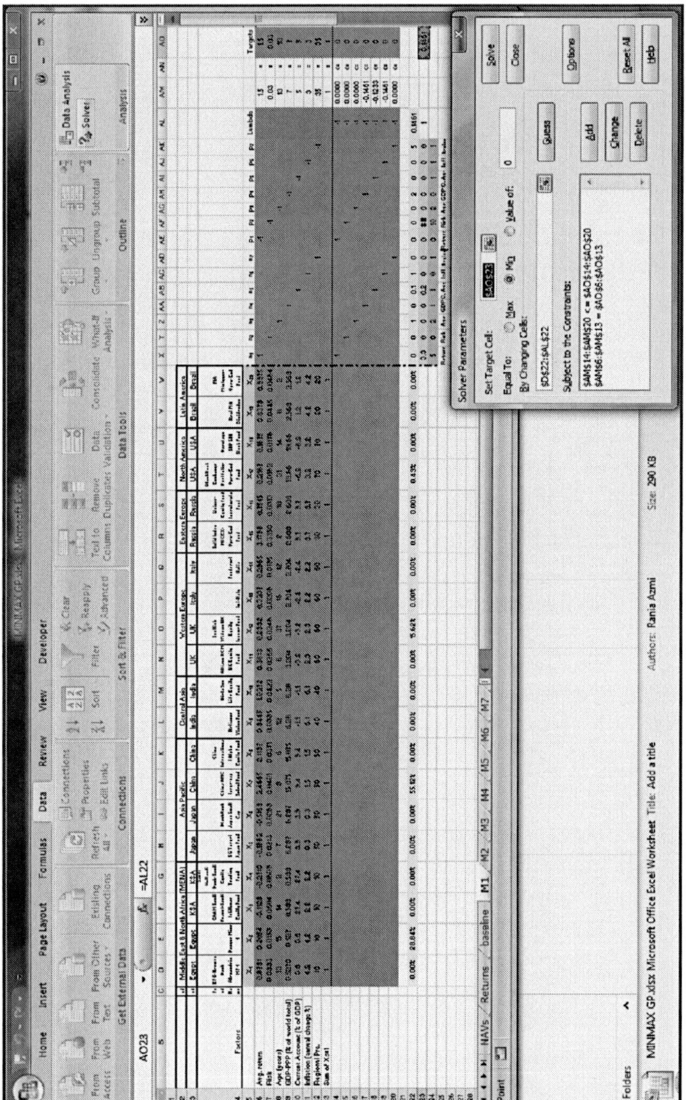

BIBLIOGRAPHY

Abdelaziz, F., Aouni, B. and El Fayedh, R. (2007). "Multi-objective Stochastic Programming for Portfolio Selection", European Journal of Operational Research, Vol. 177, pp. 1811-1823.

Alexander, G. and Resnick, B. (1985). "Using Linear and Goal Programming to Immunize Bond Portfolios", Journal of Banking & Finance, Elsevier, Vol. 9, pp. 35-54.

Allen, J., Bhattacharya, S. and Smarandache, F. (2003). "Fuzziness and Funds Allocation in Portfolio Optimisation", International Journal of Social Economics, Vol. 30, No. 5, pp. 619-632.

Amenc, N. and Le Sourd, V. (2003). Portfolio Theory and Performance Analysis, Wiley Finance, John Wiley & Sons Ltd.

Aouni, B. and La Torre, D. (2010). "A Generalized Stochastic Goal Programming Model", Applied Mathematics and Computation, Vol. 215, pp. 4347-4357.

Artikis, P. (2002). "Evaluation of Equity Mutual Funds Operating in the Greek Financial Market", Managerial Finance, Vol. 28, pp. 27-42.

Artzner, P., Delbaen, F., Eber, J-M. and Heath, D. (1999). "Coherent Measures of Risk", Mathematical Finance, Vol. 9, pp. 203-228.

Azmi, R. (2005). "Analytical Study of the Egyptian Mutual Funds Performance and its Determinants", Master's thesis, Alexandria University, Egypt.

—. (2011). "SWF Perspectives: Investment Portfolio Selection using Goal Programming: A Multiple-Objectives Framework for Practitioners and Academics", Sovereign Wealth Quarterly, January, SWF Institute, pp. 20-23.

Azmi, R. and Tamiz, M. (2010). "A Review of Goal Programming for Portfolio Selection", New Developments in Multiple Objective and Goal Programming, Lecture Notes in Economics and Mathematical Systems 638, Springer-Verlag Berlin Heidelberg, pp. 15-33.

Balbas, A., Balbas, B. and Balbas, R. (2009). "CAPM and APT Like Models with Risk Measures", Technical Report, No. 1/09, June, pp. 1-32.

Balbas, A., Balbas, R. and Mayoral, S. (2009). "Portfolio Choice and Optimal Hedging with General Risk Functions: A Simplex-Like Algorithm", European Journal of Operational Research, Vol. 192, pp. 603-620.

Bartram S. and Bodnar, G. (2009). "No Place to Hide: The Global Crisis in Equity Markets in 2008/2009", Journal of International Money and Finance, Vol. 28, pp. 1-69.

Bilbao, A., Arenas, M., Jimenez, M., Gladish, B. and Rodriguez, M. (2006). "An Extension of Sharpe's Single-Index Model: Portfolio Selection with Expert Betas", Operational Research Society, Vol. 57, pp. 1442-1451.

Bilbao, A., Arenas, M., Rodriguez, M. and Antomil, J. (2007). "On Constructing Expert Betas for Single-Index Model", European Journal of Operational Research, Vol. 183, pp. 827-847.

BIS. (2009). The Global Financial Crisis, BIS 79th Annual Report, Bank for International Settlements, June, pp. 16-36.

Bliss R., Potter M. and Schwarz C. (2008). "Performance Characteristics of Individually-Managed versus Team-Managed Mutual Funds", the Journal of Portfolio Management, Spring, pp. 110-119.

Block, S. and French, W. (2002). "The Effect of Portfolio Weighting on Investment Performance Evaluation: The Case of Actively Managed Mutual Funds", Economics and Finance, Vol. 26, pp. 16-30.

Booth, G. and Dash, G. (1977). "Bank Portfolio Management Using Non-Linear Goal Programming", the Financial Review, Vol. 14, pp. 59-69.

Byrne, P. and Lee, S. (1994). "Real Estate Portfolio Analysis Using a Spreadsheet Optimizer", Journal of Property Finance, Vol. 5, No. 4, pp. 19-31.

Caldentey, E. and Vernengo, M. (2010). "Modern Finance, Methodology and the Global Crisis", Real-World Economics Review, Issue No. 52, pp. 69-81.

Callin, S. (2008). Portable Alpha Theory and Practice: What Investors Really need to Know, John Wiley & Sons, Inc.

Carhart, M. (1997). "On Persistence in Mutual Fund Performance", the Journal of Finance, pp. 57-81.

CBE (2003). Economic Review, Research, Development and Publishing Sector, Central Bank of Egypt, Vol. 43, pp. 1-232.

—. (2009). Economic Review, Research, Development and Publishing Sector, Central Bank of Egypt, Vol. 49, pp. 1-146.

Chang, C.-T. (2007). "Efficient Structures of Achievement Functions for Goal Programming Models", Asia-Pacific Journal of Operational Research, Vol. 24, No. 6, pp. 755-764.

Charnes, A., Cooper, W. and Ferguson, R. (1955). "Optimal estimation of executive Compensation by Linear Programming", Management Science, Vol. 1, No. 1, pp. 138-151.
Chow, G. (1995). "Portfolio Selection Based on Return, Risk, and Relative Performance", Financial Analysts Journal, Vol. March-April, pp. 54-60.
Christiansen, J. and Varnes, C. (2008). "From Models to Practice: Decision Making at Portfolio Meetings", International Journal of Quality & Reliability Management, Vol. 25, No. 1, pp. 87-101.
Corrado, C. and Jordan, B. (2005). Fundamentals of Investments: Valuations & Management, third edition, McGraw-Hill Trwin.
Cremers, J.-H., Kritzman, M. and Page, S. (2005). "Optimal Hedge Fund Allocations", the Journal of Portfolio Management, Spring, pp. 70-81.
Cresson, J., Cudd, R. and Lipscomb, T. (2002). "The Early Attraction of S&P 500 Index Funds: Is Perfect Tracking Performance an Illusion?", Journal of Managerial Finance, Vol. 28, pp. 1-8.
Daniel, K., Grinblatt, M., Titman, S. and Wermers, R. (1997). "Measuring Mutual Fund Performance with Characteristic-Based Benchmarks", the Journal of Finance, Vol. 52, pp. 1035-1058.
Das, N., Kish, R., Muething, D., and Taylor, L. (2002). "Literature on Hedge Funds", Discussion Paper, Lehigh University, Pennsylvania, pp. 1-88.
Dash, G. and Kajiji, N. (2005). "A Nonlinear Goal Programming Model for Efficient Asset-Liability Management of Property-Liability Insurers", INFOR, Vol. 43, No. 2, pp. 135-156.
Davies, R., Kat, H. and Lu, S. (2005). "Fund of Hedge Funds Portfolio Selection: A Multiple Objective Approach", SSRN, pp. 1-31.
Deng, X.-T., Li, Z.-F. and Wang, S.-Y. (2005). "A Minimax Portfolio Selection Strategy with Equilibrium", European Journal of Operational Research, Vol. 166, pp. 278-292.
Deng, X.-T., Wang, S.-Y. and Xia, Y.-S. (2000). "Criteria, Models and Strategies in Portfolio Selection", Advanced Modelling and Optimization (AMO), Vol. 2, No. 2, pp. 79-103.
Dor, A., Budinger, V., Dynkin, L. and Leech, K. (2008). "Constructing Peer Benchmarks for Mutual Funds: A Style Analysis-Based Approach", the Journal of Portfolio Management, Winter, pp. 65-77.
Elton, E. and Gruber, M. (1995). Modern Portfolio Theory and Investment Analysis, Fifth Edition, John Wiley & Sons, Inc.
Fama, E. (1996). "Multifactor Portfolio Efficiency and Multifactor Asset Pricing", Financial and Quantitative Analysis, Vol. 31, pp. 441-465.

Fama, E. and French, K. (1993). "Common Risk Factors in the Returns on Stocks and Bonds", Journal of Financial Economics, Vol. 33, pp. 3-56.

Frangsmyr, T. (Ed.) (1991). "Harry M. Markowitz Autobiography", The Nobel Prizes 1990, Les Prix Nobel, Nobel Foundation, Stockholm.

Fulga, C. (2009). "Multistage Portfolio Optimization", Institute of Mathematics and Informatics, Vilnius Gediminas Technical University, Vilnius, pp. 497-501.

Gallagher, D. (2002). "Investment Manager Characteristics, Strategy and Fund Performance", Unpublished Doctoral Dissertation, School of Business, Faculty of Economics and Business, The University of Sydney, Australia.

Garcia, F., Guijarro, F., and Moya, I. (2010). "A Goal Programming Approach to Estimating Performance Weights for Ranking Firms", Computers & Operations Research, Vol. 37, pp. 1597-1609.

Gladish, B., Jones, D., Tamiz, M. and Terol, B. (2007). "An Interactive Three-Stage Model for Mutual Funds Portfolio Selection", The International Journal of Management Science, OMEGA, Vol. 35, pp. 75-88.

Gregoriou, G. (2007). Diversification and Portfolio Management of Mutual Funds, Palgrave Macmillan.

Grinblatt, M. and Titman, S. (1989). "Portfolio Performance Evaluation: Old Issues and New Insights", The Review of Financial Studies, Vol. 2, pp. 393-421.

Grinold, R. and Kahn, R. (1995). Active Portfolio Management: Quantitative Theory and Applications, Probus Publishing Company.

Hu, W. and Kercheval, A. (2007). "Portfolio Optimization for Skewed-t Returns", working paper.

Huang, X. (2008). "Mean-Semivariance Models for Fuzzy Portfolio Selection", Computational and Applied Mathematics, Vol. 217, pp. 1-8.

Hymans, C. and Mulligan, J. (1980). The Measurement of Portfolio Performance: An Introduction, Kluwer Publishing Ltd.

ICI. (2009). Investment Company Fact Book: A Review of Trends and Activity in the Investment Company Industry, Investment Company Institute, http://www.icifactbook.org, Vol. 49, pp. 1- 208.

Ignizio, J. (1978). "A Review of Goal Programming: A Tool for Multiobjective Analysis", Operational Research Society, Vol. 29, pp. 1109-1119.

—. (1985). Introduction to Linear Goal Programming Series: Quantitative Applications in the Social Sciences, SAGE University Paper 56, SAGE Publications, Inc.

Ignizio, J and Romero, C. (2003). Goal Programming. In: Bidgoli, H (Ed.), Encyclopedia of Information Systems, Academic Press, San Diego, Vol. 2, pp. 489-500.

IMF (2006). Data and Statistics, the IMF financial Data, the International Monetary Fund.

—. (2007). World Economic Outlook: Globalization and Inequality, the World Economic and Financial Surveys, the International Monetary Fund.

Inuiguchi, M. and Ramik, J. (2000). "Possibilistic Linear Programming: A Brief Review of Fuzzy Mathematical Programming and a Comparison with Stochastic Programming in Portfolio Selection Problem", Fuzzy Sets and Systems, Vol. 111, pp. 3-28.

Jensen, M. (1968). "The Performance of Mutual Funds in the Period 1945-1964", the Journal of Finance, Vol. 23, pp. 389-416.

Jobst, N.; Horniman, M.; Lucas, C. and Mitra, G. (2001). "Computational aspects of alternative portfolio selection models in the presence of discrete asset choice constraints", Journal of Quantitative Finance, Vol. 1, pp. 1-13.

Jones, D. and Tamiz, M. (2010). Practical Goal Programming, International Series in Operations Research and Management Science, Springer.

Keeney, R. (2003). Decisions with Multiple Objectives: Preferences and Value Tradeoffs, Cambridge University Press, Cambridge, Massachusetts.

Kim, J., Kim, Y. and Shin, K. (2005). "An Algorithm for Portfolio Optimization Problem", INFORMATICA, Institute of Mathematics and Informatics, Vol. 16, No. 1, pp. 93-106.

Konno, H. (2003). "Portfolio Optimization of Small Scale Fund Using Mean-Absolute Deviation Model", International Journal of Theoretical and Applied Finance, Vil. 6, pp. 403-418.

Konno, H. and Kobayashi, K. (1997). "An integrated stock-bond portfolio optimization model", Journal of Economic Dynamics and Control, Vol. 21, pp. 1427-1444.

Konno, H. and Koshizuka, T. (2005). "Mean-Absolute Deviation Model", IIE Transactions, Vol. 37, pp. 893-900.

Konno, H. and Yamazaki, H. (1991). "Mean-Absolute Deviation Portfolio Optimization and its Applications to Tokyo Stock Market", Management Science, Vol. 37, pp. 519-531.

Kooros, S. and McManis, B. (1998). "Multiattribute Optimization Model for Strategic Investment Decisions", Canadian Journal of Administrative Sciences, Vol. 15, No. 2, pp. 152-164.

Kosmidou, K. and Zopounidis, C. (2004). "Combining Goal Programming Model with Simulation Analysis for Bank Asset Liability Management", INFOR, Vol. 42, No. 3, pp. 175-187.

Kritzman, M. (2003). The Portable Financial Analyst: What Practitioners Need to Know, second edition, John Wiley & Sons, Inc.

Kumar, P. and Philippatos, G. (1979). "Conflict Resolution in Investment Decisions: Implementation of Goal Programming Methodology for Dual-Purpose Funds", Decision Sciences, Vol. 10, pp. 562-576.

Kumar, P., Philippatos, G. and Ezzell, J. (1978). "Goal Programming and Selection of Portfolio by Dual-Purpose Funds", the Journal of Finance, Vol. 33, pp. 303-310.

Lai, Y.-J. and Hwang, C.-L. (1994). "Fuzzy Multiple Objective Decision Making: Methods and Applications", Lecture Notes in Economics and Mathematical Systems, 404, Spring-Verlag.

Lasdon, L., Waren, A., Jain, A. and Ratner, M. (1976). "Design and Testing of a Generalized Reduced Gradient Code for Nonlinear Programming", Technical Report SOL 76-3, Systems Optimization Laboratory, Department of Operations Research, Stanford University, pp.1-47.

Lawler, E. and Wood, D. (1966). "Branch-And-Bound Methods: A Survey", Operations Research, Vol. 14, pp. 699-719.

Lee, S. (1972). Goal Programming for Decision Analysis, AUERBACH Publishers Inc.

Lee, S. and Chesser, D. (1980). "Goal Programming for Portfolio Selection", the Journal of Portfolio Management, Vol. 6, pp. 22-26.

Lee, S. and Lerro, A. (1973). "Optimizing the Portfolio Selection for Mutual Funds", the Journal of Finance, Vol. 28, pp. 1086-1101.

Lehmann, B., and Modest, D. (1987). "Mutual Fund Performance Evaluation: A Comparison of Benchmarks and Benchmarks Comparison", the Journal of Finance, Vol. 42, pp. 233-265.

Leon, T., Liern, V. and Vercher, E. (2002). "Viability of Infeasible Portfolio Selection Problems: A Fuzzy Approach", European Journal of Operational Research, Vol. 139, pp. 178-189.

Levary, R. and Avery, M. (1984). "On the Practical Application of Weighting Equities in a Portfolio via Goal Programming", Opsearch, Vol. 21, pp. 246-261.

Li, J. and Xu, J. (2007). "A Class of Possibilistic Portfolio Selection Model with Interval Coefficients and its Application", Fuzzy Optimal Decision Making, Vol. 6, Springer, pp. 123-137.

Mansini, R., Ogryczak, W. and Speranza, M.G. (2007). "Conditional Value at Risk and Related Linear Programming Models for Portfolio Optimization, Annals of Operations Research, Vol. 152, pp. 227-256.
Markowitz, H. (1952). "Portfolio Selection", the Journal of Finance, Vol. 7, pp. 77-91.
—. (1991). "Foundations of Portfolio Theory", the Journal of Finance, Vol. 46, pp. 469-477.
—. (1995). Portfolio Selection: Efficient Diversification of Investments, Second Edition, Blackwell Publishers.
Matallin, J., and Nieto, L. (2002). "Mutual Funds as an Alternative to Direct Stock Investment", the Journal of Applied Financial Economics, pp. 743-750.
Miller, E. (2002). "Why the Low Returns to Beta and Other Forms of Risk", the Journal of Portfolio Management, Institutional Investor, Winter, pp. 40-55.
Muhlemann, A., Lockett, A. and Gear, A. (1978). "Portfolio Modelling in Multiple-Criteria Situations Under Uncertainty", Decision Sciences, Vol. 9, pp. 612-626.
Nelder, J. and Mead, R. (1965). "A Simplex Method for Function Minimization", the Computer Journal, Vol. 7, pp. 308-313.
Ogryczak, W. (2000). "Multiple Criteria Linear Programming Model for Portfolio Selection", Annals of Operations Research, Vol. 97, pp. 143-162.
Ogryczak, W. and Ruszczynski, A. (2002). "Dual Stochastic Dominance and Quantile Risk Measures", Journal of International Transactions in Operational Research, Vol. 9, pp. 661-680.
Otten, R., and Schweitzer, M. (2002). "A Comparison between the European and the U.S. Mutual Fund Industry", Journal of Managerial Finance, Vol. 28, pp. 14-34.
Parra, M., Terol, A. and Uria, M. (2001). "A Fuzzy Goal Programming Approach to Portfolio Selection", European Journal of Operational Research, Vol. 133, pp. 287-297.
Pastor, L. (2000). "Portfolio Selection and Asset Pricing Models", the Journal of Finance, Vol. 55, pp. 179-223.
Pearson, N. (2002). Risk Budgeting: Portfolio Problem Solving with Value-at-Risk, John Wiley & Sons, Inc.
Pendaraki, K., Doumpos, M. and Zopounidis, C. (2004). "Towards a Goal Programming Methodology for Constructing Equity Mutual Fund Portfolios", Journal of Asset Management, Vol. 4, No. 6, pp. 415-428.

Pendaraki, K., Zopounidis, C. and Doumpos, M. (2005). "On the Construction of Mutual Fund Portfolios: A Multicriteria Methodology and an Application to the Greek Market of Equity Mutual Funds", European Journal of Operational Research, Vol. 163, pp. 462-481.

Peterson, J., Pietranico, P., Riepe, M., and Xu, F. (2001). "Explaining the performance of Domestic Equity Mutual Funds", Journal of Investing, Institutional Investor Inc., pp. 1-14.

Pflug, G. (2006). "Subdifferential Representations of Risk Measures", Mathematical Programming, Vol. 108, pp. 339-354.

Prakash, A., Chang, C. and Pactwa, T. (2003). "Selecting a Portfolio with Skewness: Recent Evidence from US, European, and Latin American Equity Markets", Journal of Banking & Finance, Vol. 27, pp. 1375-1390.

Raj, M., Forsyth, M., and Tomini, O. (2003). "Fund Performance in a Downside Context", Journal of Investing, Institutional Investor Inc., pp. 50-63.

Redman, A., Gullett, N., and Manakyan, H. (2000). "The Performance of Global International Mutual Fund", Journal of Financial and Strategic Decisions, Vol. 13, pp. 75-85.

Reina, L. (2005). "From Subjective Expected Utility Theory to Bounded Rationality: An Experimental Investigation on Categorization Processes in Integrative Negotiation, in Committees' Decision Making and in Decisions under Risk", doctorate book, Technische Universität Dresden.

Renwick, F. (1969). "Asset Management and Investor Portfolio Behaviour: Theory and Practice", the Journal of Finance, Vol. 24, No. 2, pp. 180-205.

Rifai, A. (1996). "A Note on the Structure of the Goal-Programming Model: Assessment and Evaluation", International Journal of Operations & Production Management, Vol. 16, pp. 40-49.

Rockafellar, R., Uryasev, S. and Zabarankin, M. (2006). "Generalized Deviations in Risk Analysis", Finance & Stochastics, Vol.10, pp. 51-74.

Romero, C. (1991). Handbook of Critical Issues in Goal Programming, Pergamon Press.

—. (2004). "A General Structure of Achievement Function for a Goal Programming Model", European Journal of Operational Research, Vol. 153, pp. 675-686.

Ross, S. (1976). "The Arbitrage Pricing Theory of Capital Asset Pricing", Journal of Economic Theory, Vol. 13, pp. 241-360.

Rostamy, A., Azar, A. and Hosseini, S. (2003). "A Mixed Integer Goal Programming (MIGP) Model for Multi-period Complex Corporate Financing Problems", Journal of Finance India, Vol. XVII, No. 2, pp. 495-509.

Schniederjans M (1995). Goal Programming: Methodology and Applications, Springer.

Scholz, H. (2007). "Refinements to the Sharpe Ratio: Comparing Alternatives for Bear Markets", Journal of Asset Management, Vol. 7, No. 5, pp. 347-357.

Sharma, H., Ghosh, D. and Sharma, D. (2007). "Credit Union Portfolio Management: An Application of Goal Interval Programming", Academy of Banking Studies Journal, Vol. 6, No.1, pp. 39-60.

Sharma, H. and Sharma, D. (2006). "A Multi-Objective Decision-Making Approach For Mutual Fund Portfolio", Journal of Business & Economics Research, Vol. 4, pp. 13-24.

Sharpe, W. (1963). "A Simplified Model for Portfolio Analysis", Management Science, January, pp.277-293.

—. (1964). "Capital Asset Prices: A Theory of Market Equilibrium under Conditions of Risk", the Journal of finance, Vol. 19, pp. 425-442.

—. (1966). "Mutual Fund Performance", Journal of Business, Vol. 39, pp. 119-138.

—. (1985). Investments, third edition, Prentice-Hall Inc.

Steuer, R., Qi, Y. and Hirschberger, M. (2007). "Suitable-Portfolio Investors, Nondominated Frontier Sensitivity, and the Effect of Multiple Objectives on Standard Portfolio Selection", Journal of Annals of Operations Research, Springer, Vol. 152, pp. 297-317.

Stone, B. and Reback, R. (1975). "Constructing a Model for Managing Portfolio Revisions", Journal of Bank Research, Vol. 6, pp. 48-60.

Sun, Q. and Yan, Y. (2003). "Skewness Persistence with Optimal Portfolio Selection", Journal of Banking and Finance, Vol. 27, pp.1111-1121.

Tamiz, M. and Azmi, R. (2010). "Mutual Funds Portfolio Selection for Emerging Market: The Case for Egypt", the Journal of Financial Decision Making (JFDM), Vol. 6, No. 2, pp. 31-40.

Tamiz, M., Azmi, R., Jones, D. (2013). "On Selecting Portfolio of International Mutual Funds using Goal Programming with Extended Factors", European Journal of Operational Research, Volume 226, Issue 3, pp. 560-576.

—. (2011). "Selecting Portfolios based on Sharpe, Treynor and Goal Programming Methodologies: Applications to Mutual Funds in the UK and Egypt", the Arab Journal of Administrative Sciences, Vol. 18, No. 3, pp. 495-514.

Tamiz, M, Hasham, R., Fargher, K. and Jones, D. (1997). "A Comparison between Goal Programming and Regression Analysis for Portfolio Selection", Lecture Notes in Economics & Mathematical Systems, Springer, Vol. 448, pp. 421-432.

Tamiz, M, Hasham, R. and Jones, D. (1996). "A Two Staged Goal Programming Model for Portfolio Selection", Lecture Notes in Economics & Mathematical Systems, Springer, Vol. 432, pp. 286-299.

Tamiz, M. and Jones, D. (1995). "A Review of Goal Programming and its Applications", Annals of Operations Research, Vol. 58, pp. 39-53.

—. (1997). "An Example of Good Modelling Practice in Goal Programming: Means for Overcoming Incommensurability", Lecture Notes in Economics and Mathematical Systems, Springer, Vol. 455, pp. 29-37.

—. (1998). "Goal Programming: Recent Developments in Theory and Practice", International Journal of Management and Systems, Vol. 14, pp. 1-16.

Tamiz, M., Jones, D. and Romero, C. (1998). "Goal Programming for Decision Making: An Overview of the Current State-of-the-Art", European Journal of Operational Research, Vol. 111, pp. 569-581.

Tektas, A., Ozkan-Gunay, E. and Gunay, G. (2005). "Asset and Liability Management in Financial Crisis", Journal of Risk Finance, Vol. 6, No. 2, pp. 135-149.

Teresiene, D. and Paskevicius, P. (2009). "Portfolio Construction and Management during the Period of Financial Crisis", Journal of Economics and Management, Vol. 14, pp. 195-201.

Travers, F. (2004). Investment Manager Analysis: A Comprehensive Guide to Portfolio Selection, Monitoring, and Optimization, Wiley Finance, John Wiley & Sons, Inc.

Treynor, J. (1965). "How to Rate Management of Investment Funds", Harvard Business Review, Vol. 43, pp. 63-73.

Tyson, E. (2007). Mutual Funds, 5th Edition, Wiley Publishing, Inc.

Vardavaki, A. and Mylonakis, J. (2007). "An Examination of Economic Factors Determining Market Returns and Explaining Portfolio Performance Management", International Bulletin of Business Administration, EuroJournals, Inc., ISSN: 1451-243X, Issue No. 2, pp. 19-28.

Volkman, D., and Wohar, M. (1995). "Determinants of Persistence in Performance of Mutual Funds", the Journal of Financial Research, pp. 30-52.

Wang, S. and Zhu, S. (2002). "On Fuzzy Portfolio Selection Problems", Fuzzy Optimization and Decision Making, Vol. 1, No. 4, pp. 361-377.
Watada, J. (1997). "Fuzzy Portfolio Selection and Its Application to Decision Making", Tatra Mountains Mathematical Publications, No. 13, pp. 219-248.
Williams, H. P. (1978). Model Building in Mathematical Programming, John Wiley & Sons.
Winston, W. (2007). Microsoft Office Excel 2007 Data Analysis and Business Modelling, Microsoft Office, Microsoft.
Woerheide, W. (1982). "Investor Response to Suggested Criteria for the Selection of Mutual Funds", the Journal of Financial and Quantitative Analysis, Vol. 17, pp. 129-137.
Wu, L., Chou, S., Yang, C. and Ong, C. (2007). "Enhanced Index Investing Based on Goal Programming", the Journal of Portfolio Management, Vol. 33, No. 3, pp. 49-56.
Yaghoobi, M. and Tamiz, M. (2006). "On Improving a Weighted Additive Model for Fuzzy Goal Programming Problems", International Review of Fuzzy Mathematics, Vol. 1, pp. 115-129.
Yu, P. (1973). "A Class of Solutions for Group Decision Problems", Management Science, Vol. 19, pp. 936-946.
Zheng, L. (1999). "Is Money Smart? A Study of Mutual Fund Investor's Fund Selection Ability", the Journal of Finance, pp. 901-933.
Zopounidis, C. and Doumpos, M. (2002). "Multi-criteria Decision Aid in Financial Decision Making: Methodologies and Literature Review", Multi-criteria Decision Analysis, Vol. 11, pp. 167-186.

About the Author

Dr. Azmi believes even the best theory has no purpose unless it is applied in a practical manner and has spent her life – maybe inadvertently – proving it. While studying in her native Egypt, the academic and practical threads that would weave through her life began to emerge. She was working for her father's family office but also teaching at her alma mater, the University of Alexandria, after coming top of her class in business administration with a specialism in finance. Here, she also worked on development projects with the European Commission. Soon Azmi was noticed by organisations including the International Finance Corporation, part of the World Bank Group, which certified her to train small and medium-sized businesses on finance and investment, and the UN Industrial Development Organisation. From here she travelled all over the world in the footsteps of Margaret Thatcher and Tony Blair on the IV Leadership Programme. Then she started her PhD in financial mathematics. "My mandate was to bridge the gap between practitioners and academics," she says. "I created a multiple-objectives portfolio optimisation model that was absolutely necessary after the crisis." The model dismisses mathematical tradition that investment portfolios have to constrain either risk or return if the other is the focus. "I wanted to have a model that takes other factors into account and works in practical ways based on the investor's needs and preferences." She now advises one of the largest sovereign wealth funds in the world and has been keynote speaker at the CERN laboratories pension risk and investment summit. "The old, traditional risk measures are no good," she says. "We cannot just rely on them as we used to, we have to be more proactive." Azmi is an activist for women's position in business, politics, and society. She has spoken for the World Bank on gender and economics and was awarded the Google Prize for "Most Interesting and Creative Work". Most recently she was designated a Woman of Influence globally by the Women Speakers Association and is creating a model to optimise gender equality in society for the renewal of the UN's Millennium Development Goals in 2015.

Key publications:

- "On Selecting Portfolio of International Mutual Funds using Goal Programming with extended factors", European Journal of Operational Research, Volume 226, Issue 3, PP. 560-576 (2013), co-authored.
- "The Multi-Dimensions of Gender Inequalities: Measuring What Did MDGs Overcome and What Dimensions Should be Addressed Post-2015?", the United Nation's Inequalities Consultation for the Millennium Development Goals post-2015, UNICEF and UN WOMEN on Global Thematic Consultation (2012).
- "SWF Perspectives: Investment Portfolio Selection using Goal Programming, Sovereign Wealth Quarterly, January, SWF Institute, pp. 20-23 (2011).
- "A Review of Goal Programming for Portfolio Selection", New Developments in Multiple Objective and Goal Programming, Lecture Notes in Economics and Mathematical Systems 638, Springer-Verlag Berlin Heidelberg, pp. 15-33 (2010), co-authored.
- "Mutual Funds Portfolio Selection for Emerging Market: The Case for Egypt", the Journal of Financial Decision Making (JFDM), Vol. 6, No. 2, pp. 31-40 (2010), co-authored.
- "Contagion within Financial Markets and Networks across the Globe: Evidence from Equity Mutual Funds during the Current Crisis", Available at SSRN: http://ssrn.com/abstract= 1691157 (2009), co-authored.
- Cooperative Finance and Sustainability After the Financial Crisis, book chapter in William Sun, Céline Louche, Roland Pérez (ed.) Finance and Sustainability: Towards a New Paradigm? A Post-Crisis Agenda (Critical Studies on Corporate Responsibility, Governance and Sustainability, Volume 2), Emerald Group Publishing Limited, pp. 233-247 (2011).
- "Gender and Financial Mathematics: Evidence from Mutual Funds Performance in one of the Emerging Markets", Proceedings of the 3rd Nordic EWM, TUCS General Publication, No. 53, pp. 23-33 (2009).
- "Globalization of Information Sharing and Modern Technologies", The NATO Advanced Research Workshop: Scientific Networking and the Global Health Network Supercourse, pp. 53-57 (2005).

INDEX